5OO BRACELETS

500 BRACELETS

An Inspiring Collection of Extraordinary Designs

LARK BOOKS

A Division of Sterling Publishing Co., Inc.

New York / London

Editor: Marthe Le Van

Art Director: Susan McBride

Cover Designer: Barbara Zaretsky

Associate Editor: Nathalie Mornu

Associate Art Director: Shannon Yokeley

Editorial Assistance: Dawn Dillingham,
Delores Gosnell

Editorial Interns: Kelly J. Johnson,
Megan S. McCarter, Metta L. Pry,
David Squires

Proofreaders: Sherry Hames,
Rebecca Guthrie

COVER
Reiko Ishiyama
Untitled, 2000

SPINE
Flora Book
Cosmic Structure, 2001

BACK COVER, TOP LEFT
Carol-lynn Swol
Spirograph Bracelet, Red, 2004

BACK COVER, TOP RIGHT
Mizuko Yamada
Tactile Bracelet, 2000

BACK COVER, BOTTOM LEFT
Marguerite Manteau Chiang
Blocks, 2002

BACK COVER, BOTTOM RIGHT
Françoise A. Sands
Untitled, 2002

FRONT FLAP
K. Dana Kagrise
Ritual # 3, 2004

BACK FLAP
Julie A. Matheis
Repose Collection: Cuffs, 2002

TITLE PAGE
Erik Urbschat
Unrund, 2000

OPPOSITE
Nina Basharova
Milky Way & Black Hole, 2004

Library of Congress Cataloging-in-Publication Data

LeVan, Marthe.
  500 bracelets : an inspiring collection of extraordinary designs / Marthe
LeVan.
      p. cm.
  Includes index.
  ISBN 1-57990-480-7 (pbk.)
  1. Bracelets--Catalogs. I. Title. II. Title: Five hundred bracelets.
NK7422.3.L48 2005
739.27'8--dc22

                                                                2005016030

10 9 8 7 6 5

Published by Lark Books, A Division of
Sterling Publishing Co., Inc.
387 Park Avenue South, New York, N.Y. 10016

© 2005, Lark Books

Distributed in Canada by Sterling Publishing,
c/o Canadian Manda Group, 165 Dufferin Street
Toronto, Ontario, Canada M6K 3H6

Distributed in the United Kingdom by GMC Distribution Services,
Castle Place, 166 High Street, Lewes, East Sussex, England BN7 1XU

Distributed in Australia by Capricorn Link (Australia) Pty Ltd.,
P.O. Box 704, Windsor, NSW 2756 Australia

The works represented are the original creations of the contributing artists.
All artists retain copyrights on their individual works, except as noted.

If you have questions or comments
about this book, please contact:
Lark Books
67 Broadway
Asheville, NC 28801
(828) 253-0467

Manufactured in China

ISBN 13: 978-1-57990-480-7
ISBN 10: 1-57990-480-7

For information about custom editions, special sales, premium and
corporate purchases, please contact Sterling Special Sales Department
at 800-805-5489 or specialsales@sterlingpub.com.

CONTENTS

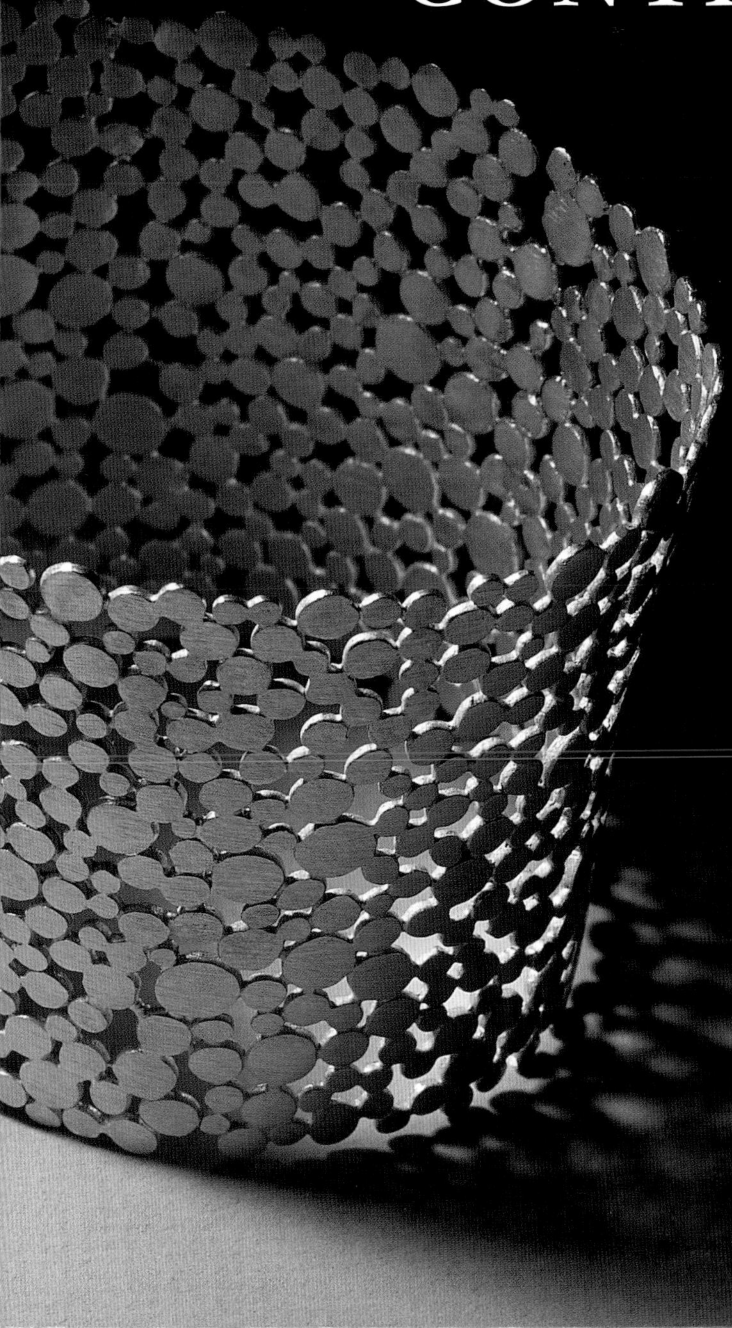

Juror's Statement

In judging this book, I selected a collection of 500 bracelets from approximately 3,000 entries over the course of three days. This process brought up a lot of questions for me. As a general rule, I never judge a piece of jewelry on its own. In order to evaluate an artist's ability, I prefer to see a full body of work. A single extraordinary piece could possibly be a stroke of luck. As a juror, I am unable to communicate with the artist about the work. I could say that a great piece of jewelry should be able to stand on its own, which is true, yet I would like to understand the relationship between the maker and his or her work, assuming that there is a relationship beyond the fact that it was made by the artist. How does the work reflect aspects of the maker? How did the piece come to its resolution? Insight into the process might influence my perception of the piece.

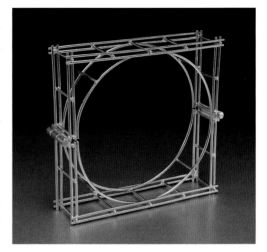

Ben Neubauer
Untitled, 2004

My experience of and exposure to jewelry has given me knowledge and insight, but this information can be a burden. One artist's early work in a specific genre may have been executed better and with more originality than more recent, similar work by a different artist in that genre. The question of authenticity and originality becomes an issue, and it is obvious for me that jewelers need to know the history of the medium to avoid creating derivative work.

How do I judge a great concept, a fresh style, an interesting angle, when the execution of the piece is technically weak? Does such a piece deserve inclusion on the merit of its idea alone for its potential to inspire readers? How will others view such a selection? What is the message? Instead of selecting a bracelet on its own, shouldn't I be forming a more holistic assessment of it with regard to how it works with the body? Since the notion of the bracelet is such a broad category, we must expand our minds to grasp the size of the ornament and what it covers.

While jurying the collection, I often found myself thinking about what would be good for the book. Instead of only selecting bracelets that caught my eye, I considered how the book would look as a whole, as a document, as an anthology. This brought up the question: If a piece is only good for a book, will it last? I found myself being aware of both of these thoughts and my selections may indicate this.

In the end, I was very inspired by the endless possibilities of expressing historical references. After all, we are also our past. The ability of artists to reinvent and reinterpret is unbelievable.

Charon Kransen

Introduction

500 Bracelets: An Inspiring Collection of Extraordinary Designs. What makes this collection inspiring? What makes the designs extraordinary? I know what I think, but why don't you decide? Every answer you come up with will be valid because your appreciation of and reaction to handmade jewelry is just that—yours. With this introduction, I aim to raise more questions that you can use to enhance your enjoyment of this collection.

Like rings, the familiar form of the bracelet is a circle or cylinder, but as you will see, the concept of what defines a bracelet is open to infinite interpretations. One would expect a multitude of metalsmiths to use the bracelet as a means of expression, but their contribution to the field is hardly exclusive. Knitters, beaders, wood carvers, ceramicists, and other artists join them in a collection that is astonishingly diverse. Personal notions of beauty, humor, poetry, sensuality, playfulness, and austerity have been realized as bracelets. They each embody a moment frozen in time, the instant when the artist stopped transforming the materials and pronounced his or her work complete and ready for you, the viewer.

Monica Schmid
Sculpture Bracelet, 2004

As you browse this collection, pause on a piece that draws your attention. What emotions does it provoke? Can you imagine wearing it? The scale of the featured pieces ranges from thin wisps of wire to colossal forged cuffs to bracelets that wind their way from the fingertips to the shoulder. As you gaze from piece to piece, consider the fit of the form. Would the bracelet curl snugly around the wrist or move freely up and down the forearm? How do you imagine a bracelet's size and weight affecting the body as it is worn? Would physical movement be restricted, enhanced, or altered in any way? As you notice multiple bracelets being worn together, observe how their shapes interact. If only a single component were worn, would the design be as strong or would the concept lose meaning? As the viewer, you are entitled to decide if these qualities are intriguing and expressive or unreasonable and inconvenient.

Jewelers are full of surprises and often rely on the unexpected. While enjoying this dynamic collection, I encourage you to ask questions and trust your answers. Allow the bracelets to speak to you in a way that is personal and profound.

Marthe Le Van

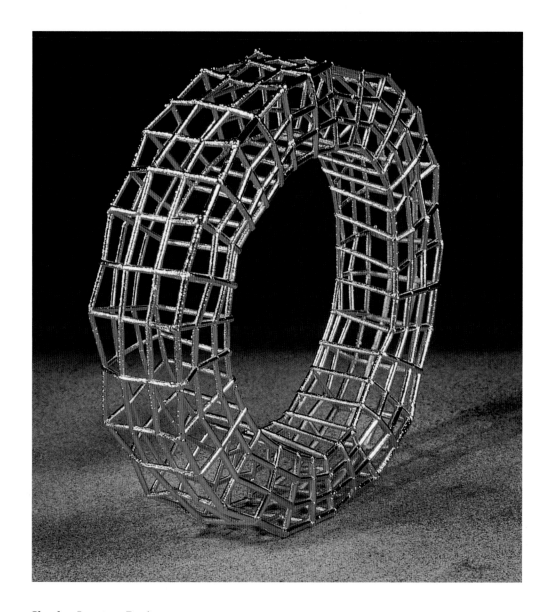

Charles Lewton-Brain

Cage Bracelet B 291, 2001

13 x 5 x 3 cm
Stainless steel, copper, 24-karat gold
plate; fusion welded, electroformed
PHOTO BY ARTIST

Emanuela Zaietta
Reflex of Light, 2004
40 x 10 x 10 cm
18-karat gold
PHOTO BY FEDERICO CAVICCHIOLI

9

Todd Reed

Cluster Bracelet, 2001

7 x 8 x 6.5 cm
18-karat yellow gold, 22-karat yellow gold, silver,
raw diamond cubes, patina; forged, hand fabricated,
hollow formed, pierced, hammer set
PHOTO BY AZAD

This bracelet has more than 1,200 geometric components, yet
seems to have an organic life. The contrast between the soft
form and hard angles creates an inviting tension. **Todd Reed**

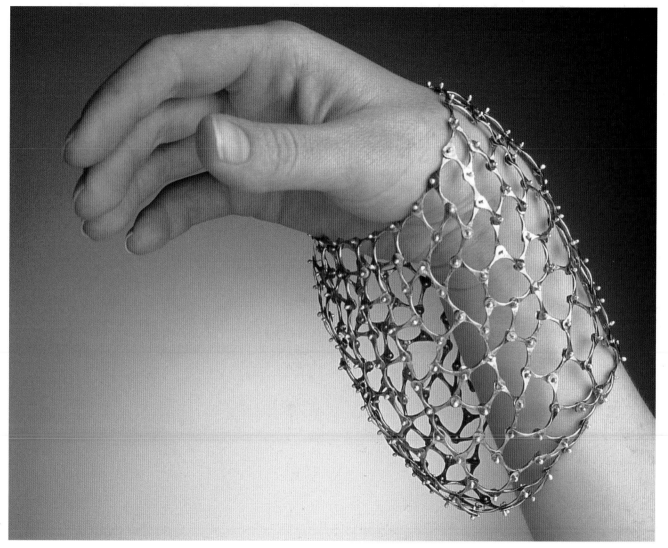

Kristine Bolhuis

Mesh System Bracelet—Hexagonal, 2002

Fully extended, 10 x 9 x 9 cm
Brass, sterling silver; forged, hand fabricated, riveted
PHOTO BY JOHN GUILLEMIN

Jan Mandel

Poignet Too Transformation Cuff, 1999

7 x 20.3 x 15.2 cm
14-karat gold, 24-karat gold, stainless steel,
seed pearls; hand fabricated, fused
PHOTO BY DOUG YAPLE

Wendy Yothers

Untitled, 2002

3 x 2 x 8 cm
18-karat gold, sterling silver;
hand fabricated, cast

PHOTO BY DICK DUANE
PRIVATE COLLECTION

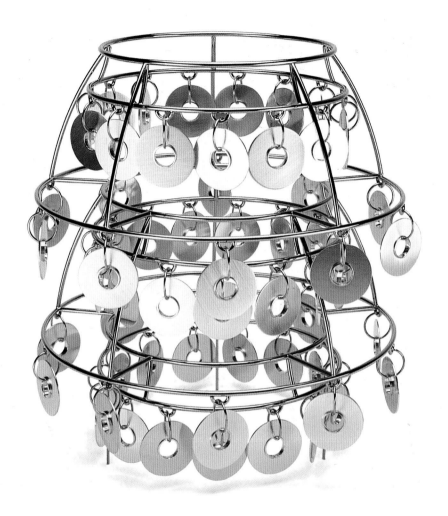

Rachelle Thiewes

Shimmer, 2002

11.5 x 10.5 x 10.5 cm
18-karat palladium white gold, silver; fabricated
PHOTO BY ARTIST
PRIVATE COLLECTION

I have long been intrigued by the brilliant white light that bathes the desert where I live. Working with visual ideas of white on white, I am able to achieve a semblance of this shimmering light by using the bright, reflective surface of polished white gold in combination with the softer surface of satined silver. **Rachelle Thiewes**

Tomoyo Hiraiwa
Do and *Sei (Motion* and *Calm)*, 2003
Each, 14 x 12 cm in diameter
Sterling silver
PHOTO BY ARTIST

Inni Pärnänen
Untitled, 2004

1.8 x 2.5 x 8.5 cm
Sterling silver; etched, soldered
PHOTO BY ARTIST

Michael Carberry

Man Made, 2003

Largest, 8 x 9 x 0.3 cm
Fine silver; hand fabricated, forged
PHOTO BY JOËL DEGEN
COLLECTION OF BRIGHTON + HOVE MUSEUM + ART GALLERY,
EAST SUSSEX, UNITED KINGDOM

My work reflects the process of its construction, allowing the surface qualities produced to trace their own development. Hammer and file marks are not removed, creating a visual reference to illustrate the techniques and physical properties of the work. **Michael Carberry**

Evan H. Larson
Evolution Ring, 2003
8.9 x 8.9 x 15.2 cm
Copper; fold formed
PHOTO BY ARTIST

Anna Heindl

Pearl Save, 2000

8 x 9 x 2 cm
18-karat white gold, black pearls

PHOTO BY MANFRED WAKOLBINGER
COLLECTION OF ANSELM KIEFER

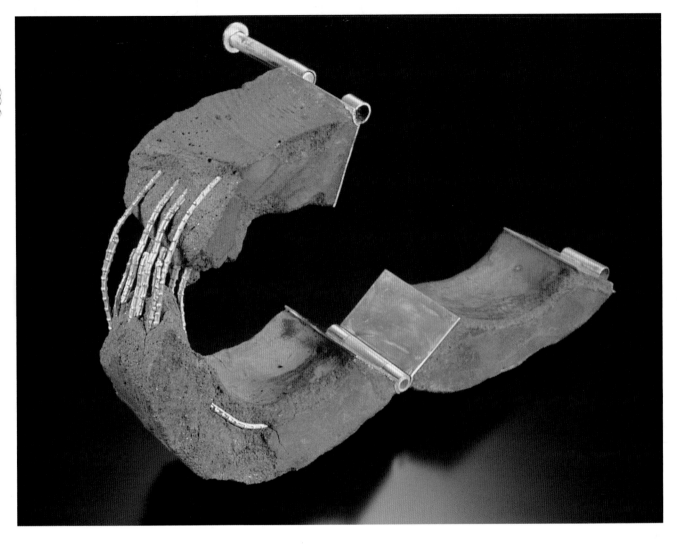

McIrvin Field-Sloan

Crushing Me with Love, 2004

9 x 10.5 x 3.3 cm
Concrete, sterling silver; cast, hand fabricated
PHOTO BY ROBERT DIAMANTE

Gundula Papesch
Pebble Bracelet, 2004
11 x 16 cm
Pebbles, silver; hand fabricated
PHOTO BY GRAZIELLA ANTONINI

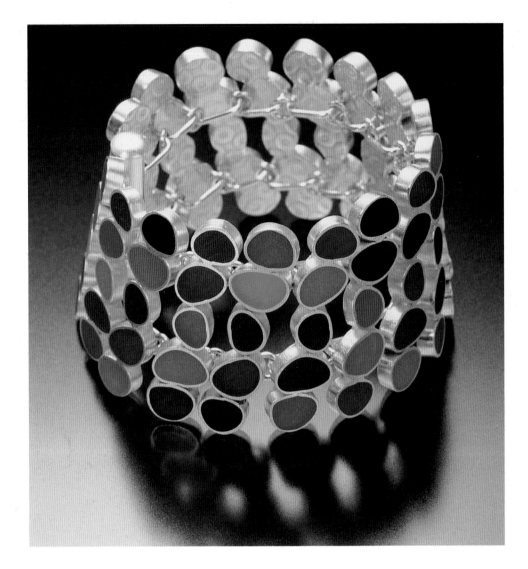

Lulu Smith

Bauble Cuff in Calm Earths, 2003

4 x 18 x 0.5 cm
Raw artist pigments, resin, sterling silver;
fabricated, cast
PHOTO BY DOUGLAS YAPLE

Unlike rings and necklaces, which traditionally are used to mark passages or rituals, bracelets are ornaments and armor. My cuff bracelets are adornment to fortify the arms with simple bold shapes and exotic use of color, each one exploring a different emotive color range. **Lulu Smith**

Zuzana Rudavska

Colorful Bracelet II, 2003

14 x 7.6 x 7.6 cm
Red coral, hematite, topaz, turquoise,
crystals, copper; crocheted
PHOTO BY GEORGE ERML
PRIVATE COLLECTION

Lauren Schlossberg

Untitled, 2003

5 x 18 x 2.5 cm
Sterling silver tube beads, sterling silver, copper, epoxy
resin, pigment, glass seed beads over wooden spheres;
fabricated, oxidized, inlaid, hand woven
PHOTO BY HAP SAKWA

Deborah Lozier

Folded Flower Bracelet in Blue, 1999

11 x 11 x 2 cm
Enamel, copper; anticlastic raising,
welded, torch fired, fold formed
PHOTO BY ERIC SMITH
COURTESY OF FACÈRÈ JEWELRY ART GALLERY,
SEATTLE, WASHINGTON

People often think this series of bracelets is made out of clay and are surprised to find out the truth after picking one up. But metal has many clay-like qualities. It simply needs the hammer to translate for the touch of the hand, and some mindful observation to understand how to go about it. Deborah Lozier

Tracy Chong

All Buttoned Up, 2004
Each, 8.4 x 8.4 x 2.2 cm
Wool, dye, buttons, magnets; wet felted,
hand stitched, dry felted
PHOTO BY ARTIST

Jürgen Lehl
Untitled, 2003
9 x 9 x 9 cm
Cotton, indigo; tie dyed
PHOTO BY EVA TAKAMINE

Giovanna Imperia

Flexibility—Shapeable Bracelet, 2004

6.4 x 17.8 cm
Coated copper wire, sterling silver;
hand woven, hand fabricated
PHOTO BY JACK B. ZILKER

This bracelet can be worn
anywhere on the arm by simply
unfolding it and reshaping it.
This is part of a recurring series
of work where the wearer is
given complete flexibility to
change the appearance of a
piece, making it unique
to her and the current mood.
Giovanna Imperia

Hsueh-Ying Wu

Emarginate Bracelet, 2004

3 x 24 x 0.1 cm
Stainless steel mesh, sterling silver;
hand fabricated
PHOTO BY CHIU CHIN-TING

Akiko Ban

The Light, 2000

9.5 x 8 x 5 cm
Sterling silver; oxidized
PHOTO BY FEDERICO CAVICCHIOLI

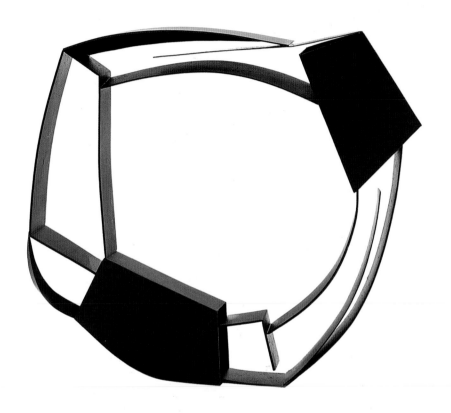

Mari Funaki

Untitled, 2004

9 x 10 x 8 cm
Mild steel; heat colored, fabricated

PHOTO BY TERENCE BOGUE
COURTESY OF GALLERY FUNAKI,
MELBOURNE, AUSTRALIA

Christel van der Laan

Priceless Bangle, 2004

15 x 15 x 15 cm
Polypropylene swing tags; woven
PHOTO BY ROBERT FRITH

My goal was to create something that is surprising and beautiful, but also thought provoking at a conceptual level. **Christel van der Laan**

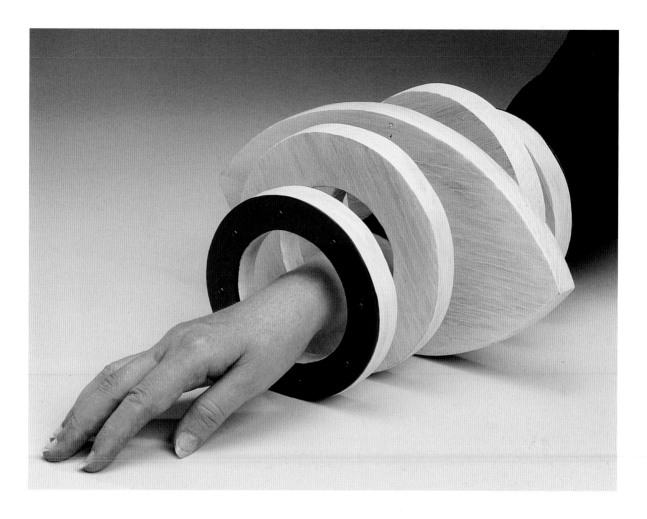

Trever Welch

Perception: The Eye, 2004

Total dimension, 15.5 x 27.1 x 10.5 cm
Wood, whitewash, color-changing paint, brass;
constructed, cut, sanded, nailed
PHOTO BY GARY POLLMILLER

Arthur David Hash

Puddle Series Bracelet, 2004

23 x 23 x 10 cm
Two-part plastic, dye
PHOTO BY ARTIST

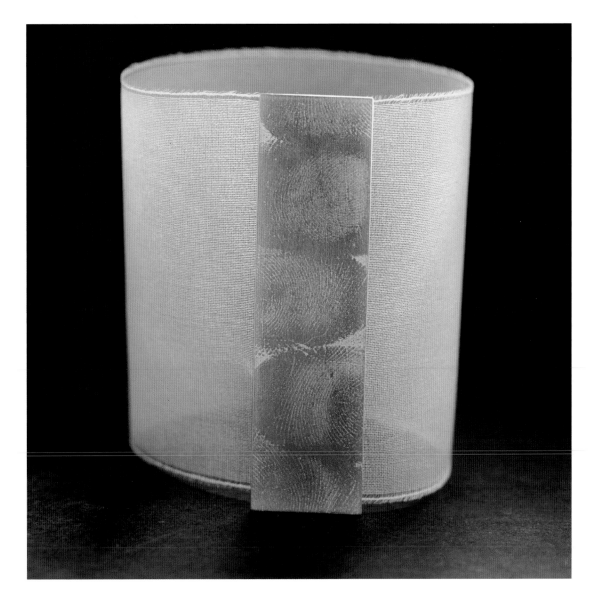

Helena Sandström

Jewelry for a Broken Arm, 2000

6.5 x 5.5 cm in diameter
Silk organdy, silver; hand fabricated, etched

PHOTO BY NIKLAS PALMKLINT
COLLECTION OF THE RHÖSS MUSEUM, GOTHENBERG, SWEDEN

Annie Pennington

Eggshell Bracelet, 2004

24.1 x 24.1 x 0.8 cm
Wood, acrylic paint, eggshells, dye; glued
PHOTO BY GARY POLLMILLER
PRIVATE COLLECTION

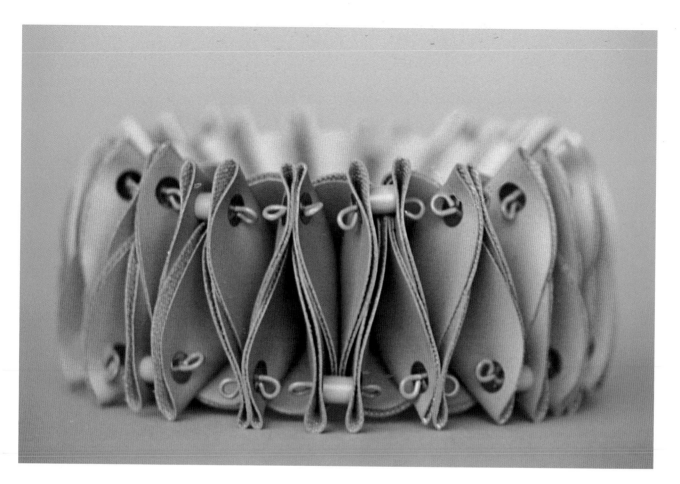

Jeanet Metselaar
Untitled, 2003
5 x 11 x 4 cm
Synthetic material
PHOTO BY HANS KOSTERINK

Joni L. Johnson

Forged Bracelet, 2001

5 x 6 x 6 cm
Sterling silver; scored, folded, hand forged
PHOTO BY JAMES BEARDS PHOTOGRAPHY

Jennifer Wells-Dickerson
Voluptuous, 2003
9 x 11 x 3 cm
Sterling silver; hand fabricated
PHOTO BY MARTY DOYLE

Carol-lynn Swol

Book Bracelet, 2003

11.4 x 11.4 x 7.6 cm

Tyvek, dye, thread; machine sewn

PHOTO BY KEVIN MONTAGUE AND MICHAEL CAVANAGH

Yeonkyung Kim
Bracelet, 2000
12 cm in diameter
Plastic
PHOTO BY ARTIST

Steven Brixner

Large Coiled Bracelet, 1977

6.4 x 7.9 x 7.9 cm
Sterling silver, fine silver; woven
(coiled basketry technique)

PHOTO BY ARTIST
COLLECTION OF MINT MUSEUM OF CRAFT + DESIGN,
CHARLOTTE, NORTH CAROLINA

Billie Jean Theide

White Ruin, 2003

8.3 cm in diameter
Sterling silver; cast, fabricated
PHOTO BY ARTIST

Mia Maljojoki

Seven Sisters, 2000

Each, 15 x 4 x 15 cm
Copper, enamel, rubber, fabric,
flock; hand fabricated, cast

PHOTO BY DEAN POWELL
COURTESY OF MOBILIA GALLERY,
CAMBRIDGE, MASSACHUSETTS

Roquin Gervot

Calyx, 2004

33 x 54 x 54 cm
Watercolor paper, handmade paper,
colored pencil, clear acrylic, white
glue, paste wax; hand sculpted,
hand fabricated, hand buffed
PHOTO BY ARTIST

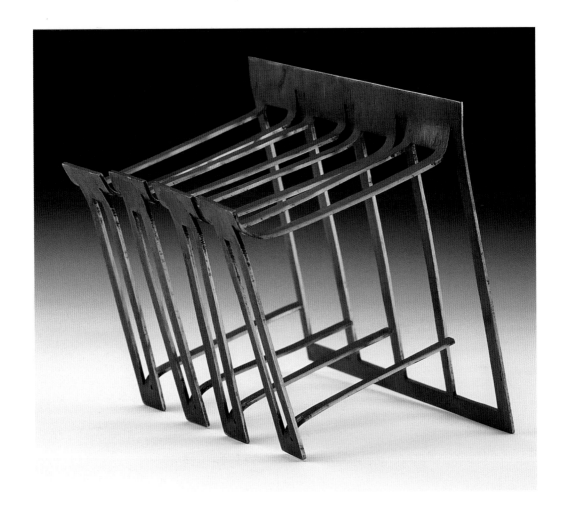

Nathan Poglein

Rectangular Dissection, 2004

10 x 8.7 x 10 cm
Copper, patina
PHOTO BY JEFFREY SABO

Susan R. Ewing
Prague Star Series: Bracelet III, 1999
16.5 x 12.5 x 4 cm
Sterling silver; hand fabricated, oxidized
PHOTO BY MARTIN TUMA

Ronda Coryell

Waves of Pearls, 2002

Each, 7.6 cm in diameter
18-karat gold, white pearls, silver pearls, black pearls;
hand fabricated, hand hammered
PHOTOS BY GEORGE POST
PRIVATE COLLECTION

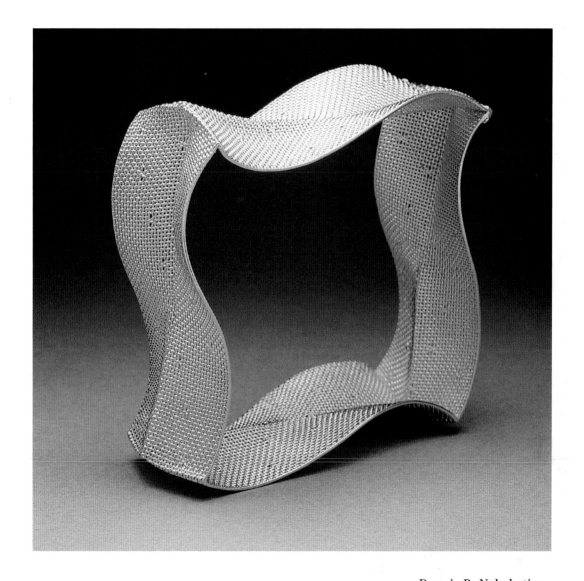

Dennis R. Nahabetian
Wave, 1998
8.9 x 8.9 x 3.2 cm
Copper, gilding
PHOTO BY ARTIST

Yasuki Hiramatsu

Bracelet, 2001

9.8 x 8.6 x 3.5 cm
24-karat yellow gold, gold leaf, epoxy resin
PHOTO BY STEVE MANN
COURTESY OF LESLEY CRAZE GALLERY, LONDON, ENGLAND

Sonia Morel

Untitled, 2002

8 x 9 x 9 cm
18-karat gold; hand fabricated,
soldered, laminated

PHOTO BY THIERRY ZUFFEREY

Stefano Marchetti

Untitled, 2000

8 x 8 x 7 cm
18-karat red gold

PHOTO BY ROBERTO SORDI
COURTESY OF MUSEUM OF ART AND
DESIGN, NEW YORK, NEW YORK

Jennifer Wells-Dickerson

Outside In, 2004

8 x 9 x 2 cm
22-karat gold, sterling silver;
hand fabricated, laminated
PHOTO BY MARTY DOYLE

A line: such a simple thing. Yet it can combine with many other lines to create a complex language of form and style. Jewelry should be a beautiful object when not adorning the body, and it should become activated when placed on the body. I consider the piece incomplete until it is worn, when the full context of its concept should become evident to the viewer and wearer. The lines, curves, angles, shapes, and dimensions must correspond harmoniously to the body. These lines should never be arbitrary.
Jennifer Wells-Dickerson

Lori Hawke

Door Plate Bracelets, 2003

Each, 6.5 x 7 x 7 cm
Door plate, photo, resin, lens, enamel
PHOTOS BY JOHN DOWLING

Kiff Slemmons

Wrist Flick, 1999

3.5 x 7 x 0.5 cm
Silver, photographs, mica; hand fabricated
PHOTO BY ROD SLEMMONS

Reiko Ishiyama

Untitled, 2000

13 x 14 x 9 cm
Sterling silver; pierced, sandpaper
finished, riveted, oxidized
PHOTO BY RALPH GABRINER

By sawing a spiral into a flat piece of metal and riveting the two ends together, suddenly, like a blossom, the entire piece opens up and takes its final shape. **Reiko Ishiyama**

Karl Fritsch
Untitled, 2003

7 x 10 x 1 cm
Sterling silver; cast, oxidized
PHOTO BY ARTIST

Beate Klockmann

Bracelet in Form of a Watch, 2004

17 x 2.5 x 1 cm

18-karat gold, glass

PHOTO BY ARTIST

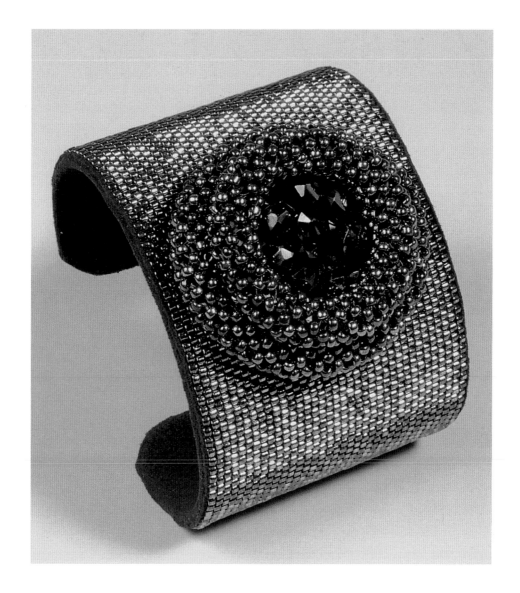

Christine Marie Noguere

Solar Flare, 2004

6.3 x 6.3 x 5.1 cm
Japanese glass cylinder seed beads, faceted garnets,
rubber rings, brass blank, Ultrasuede; off-loom bead
woven using peyote stitch and right angle weave, sewn
PHOTO BY PHIL POPE

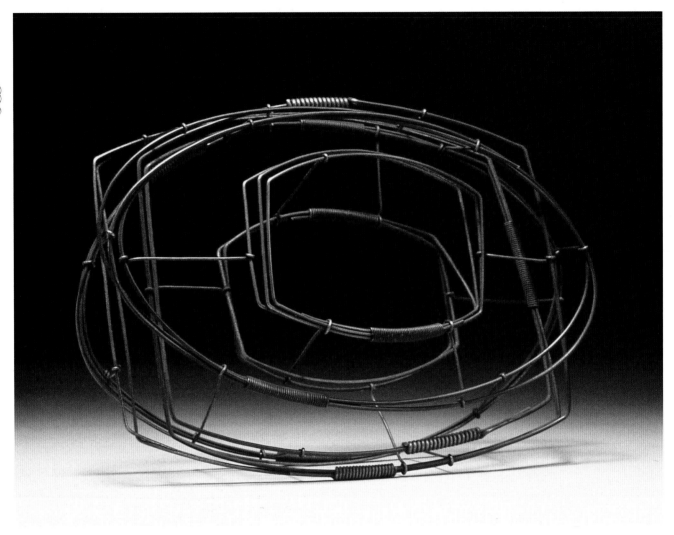

Donna D'Aquino

Wire Bracelet #83, 2002

14 x 19.7 x 7.6 cm
Steel; hand fabricated
PHOTO BY ARTIST

Using a found piece of steel as the basic structure, I have formed this simple band into a very wearable piece of jewelry. My goal was not to change its unrefined quality, but to announce it by adding a diamond and gold as a contrast. Peg Fetter

Peg Fetter

Tension Bracelet with Diamond, 2003

5 x 8 x 1 cm
Steel, 14-karat gold, diamond; forged, fabricated, tube set, heat beaded, heat oxidized, waxed
PHOTO BY DON CASPER

Annie Pennington

Autumn's Embrace, 2004

29 x 16 x 15 cm
Copper, patina; fold formed,
soldered

PHOTO BY GARY POLLMILLER
PRIVATE COLLECTION

Jane Adam

Oval Bangles, 2001

Average, 6 x 6 x 5 cm
Aluminum, dye; anodized, crazed

PHOTO BY JOËL DEGEN
COURTESY OF VELVET DA VINCI,
SAN FRANCISCO, CALIFORNIA

Nel Linssen

Flower, 2003

Each, 2 x 9 cm in diameter
Paper; folded
PHOTO BY PETER BLIEK

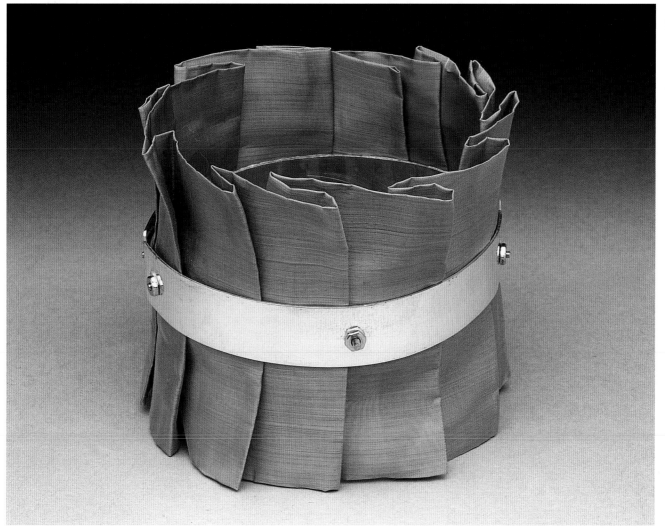

Stephane Threlkeld

Flirtation, 2003

6.5 x 7.5 x 7.5 cm
Stainless steel mesh, sterling
silver, stainless steel nuts
and bolts; cut, manipulated,
assembled
PHOTO BY GEORGE POST

Heather Bayless
Jingle Bangle, 2002
5 x 40 x 33 cm
Titanium, aluminum, sterling silver;
fabricated, riveted, anodized
PHOTO BY JEFF SABO

Inspired by botanicals, this piece celebrates the musical quality of flowers in a breeze. The titanium allows for a chiming sound as the wearer moves and the components strike each other. **Heather Bayless**

Jennifer Hall

Untitled, 2004

7.9 x 7.9 x 0.3 cm
Copper, watercolor
paints, colored pencil;
electroformed, hand
fabricated, riveted

PHOTO BY DOUG YAPLE

Julie A. Matheis

Repose Collection: Cuffs, 2002

Each, 0.2 x 7.5 cm in diameter
Feathers, thread; bound
PHOTO BY MARTY DOYLE
COURTESY OF SIENNA GALLERY,
LENOX, MASSACHUSETTS

I have altered the real qualities and symbolic role of this ancient material so these semi-plumes become a series of unnatural, colorless, and frail rings. In a subtle way, these silenced feathers propose questions regarding contemporary rituals and provide evidence of the vulnerable and impaired duality in which man and nature coexist. Julie A. Matheis

Margaret McCombs
Felt Bracelet, 2004
12.5 x 12.5 x 6.75 cm
Wool; wet felted, needle felted
PHOTO BY ARTIST

Kathleen Lamberti

Ruffle Bracelet, 2003

1.3 x 3.8 x 17.8 cm
Sterling silver, ribbon; hand fabricated, stitched
PHOTO BY HAP SAKWA

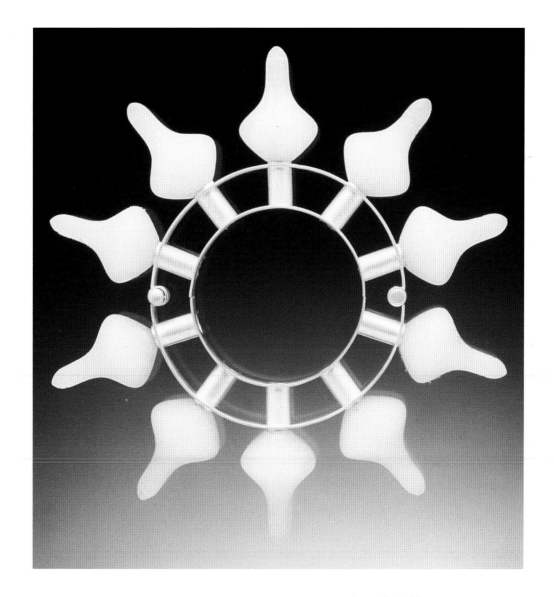

Mia Maljojoki

Anemone, 2000

18 x 3 x 18 cm
Silver, silicone rubber; hand fabricated,
computer modeled, cast

PHOTO BY DEAN POWELL
COURTESY OF MOBILIA GALLERY,
CAMBRIDGE, MASSACHUSETTS

Jennifer L. Sholtis
Constrict Brace I, 2002

14.6 x 14.2 x 1.9 cm
Epoxy resin; CAD/CAM rapid prototyped, stereolithography
PHOTO BY ARTIST

Sonja Bischur
Untitled, 1997

Detail, 9 cm in diameter
Acrylic; cut, bent, matte finished
PHOTOS BY ARTIST

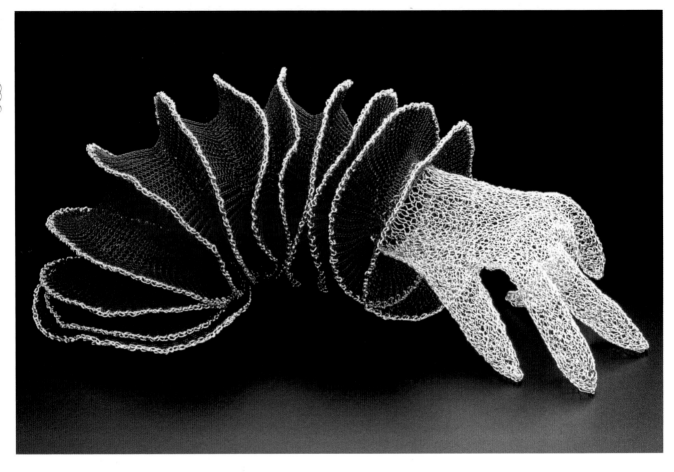

Arline Fisch

Bracelet and Glove, 1999

52 x 13 x 13 cm
Coated copper wire, fine silver; machine
knitted, hand knitted, crocheted
PHOTO BY WILLIAM GULLETTE
COLLECTION OF SMITHSONIAN ART MUSEUM'S
RENWICK GALLERY, WASHINGTON, DC

Christel van der Laan

At Any Price, 2004

17 x 17 x 4.5 cm
Ivory beads, nylon swing tags, dye; woven
PHOTO BY ROBERT FRITH

The aim behind this work is to make
a powerful statement about the value
we place on the life of a noble creature
for the sake of adornment.
Christel van der Laan

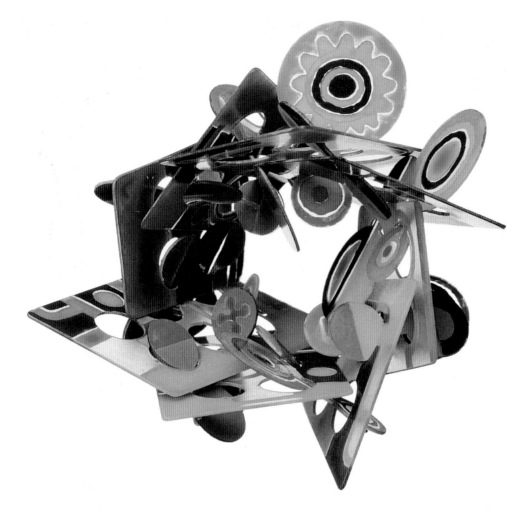

Svenja John
Bugi, 1996

7 x 8 cm in diameter
Polycarbonate; hand fabricated, hand colored
PHOTO BY JÖRG FAHLENKAMP

Felieke van der Leest

Stripey Animal Bracelets, 2003

Each, 12.5 x 10 x 4.5 cm

Yarns, silver; crocheted, fabricated

PHOTO BY EDDO HARTMANN

In each hoof of the animal is a small silver ball. The bracelet jingles like little bells. **Felieke van der Leest**

Tina Tvedt
Life Buoy for an Arm 1, 2004

12 x 10 x 10 cm
Polyester; sewn
PHOTO BY STEN MAGNE KLANN

Jessica Morrison

Yellow (left); *Blue and Yellow* (right), 2004

Each, 3.5 x 10 x 9.5 cm
Fine silver, 24-karat fine gold, sterling silver, enamel; fused
PHOTO BY TERENCE BOGUE

Jodi Johnson

Dentalium Shell Bracelet, 2004

12.5 x 12.5 x 0.6 cm
Sterling silver, 18-karat gold; fabricated, cast
PHOTO BY JAMES CHAN

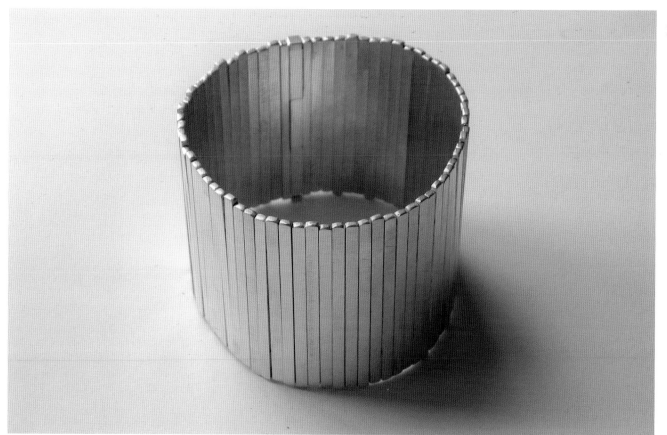

Ike Jünger
Untitled, 1993
5.5 x 6 cm
Sterling silver; hand fabricated
PHOTO BY ARTIST

Kayo Saito

Layer Bracelet, 2004

Each, 10 x 12 x 10 cm
Silver, plastic fiber,
dye, chrome; cut
PHOTO BY ARTIST

Elena Spanò

Refraction, 2004

10 x 10 x 1.5 cm
18-karat gold, thermoplastic
PHOTO BY FEDERICO CAVICCHIOLI

Water creates another dimension, and its duality is fascinating, as it asks to be experienced and that you enter its world, which is light, transparent, full of movement, where outlines are only suggested, never clear. Water embraces you, and plays with you, showing the exciting effects of light...Water is alive.
Elena Spanò

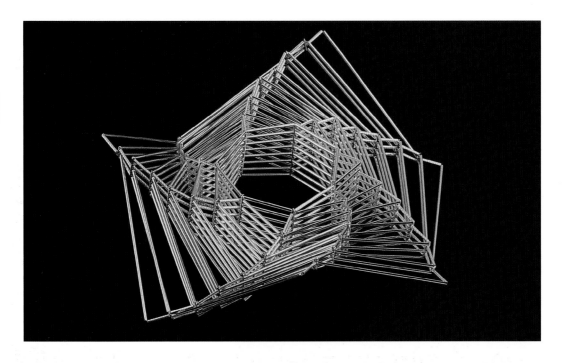

Flora Book

Cosmic Structure, 2001

7.5 x 15 x 15 cm
Sterling silver; woven
PHOTOS BY ROGER SCHREIBER

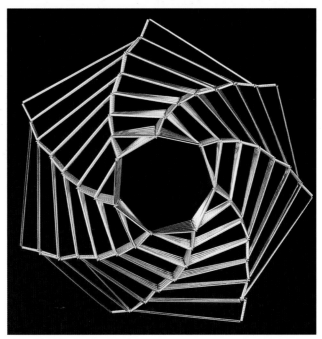

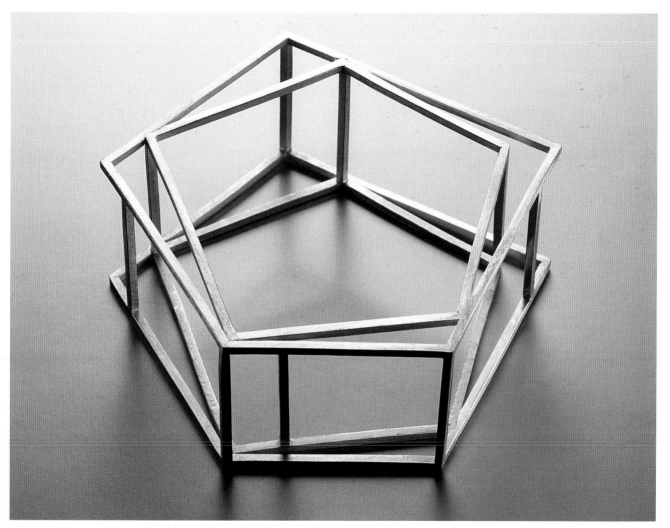

Babette von Dohnanyi
Pentagon, 1998
9 x 8 x 3 cm
Sterling silver; soldered, inscribed
PHOTO BY FEDERICO CAVICCHIOLI

Marguerite Manteau Chiang

Blocks, 2002

22.9 x 2.5 x 2.5 cm
Sterling silver, nickel silver, 18-karat gold;
hand fabricated, rough filed
PHOTO BY HAP SAKWA

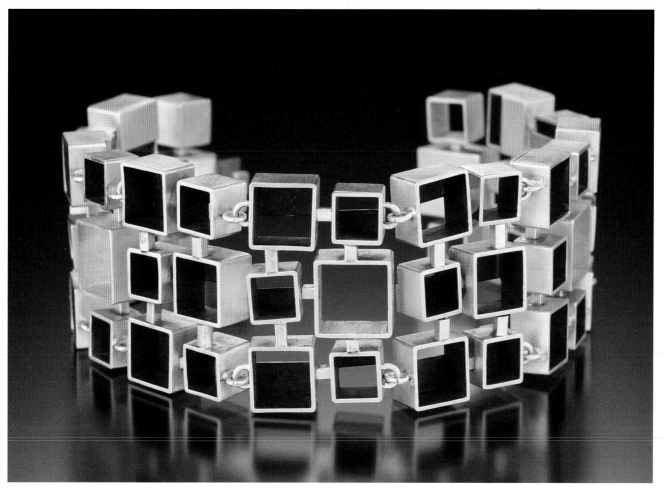

Hilary Hachey
Bauhaus Bracelet II, 2004

17.5 x 3 x 0.5 cm
Sterling silver; hand fabricated, oxidized
PHOTO BY HAP SAKWA

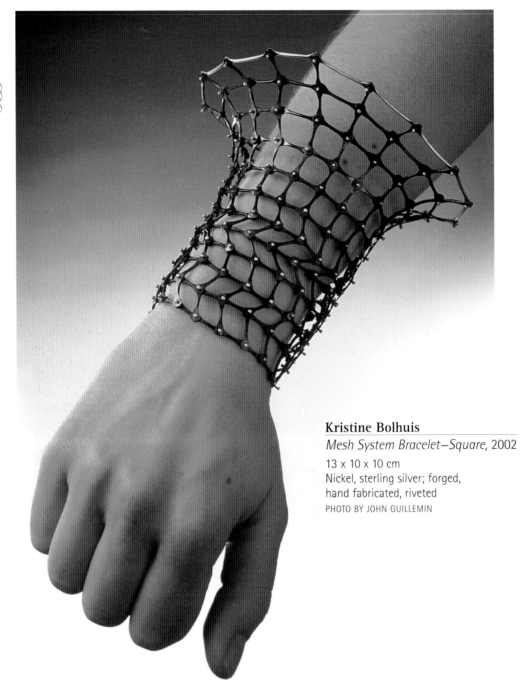

Kristine Bolhuis
Mesh System Bracelet—Square, 2002
13 x 10 x 10 cm
Nickel, sterling silver; forged,
hand fabricated, riveted
PHOTO BY JOHN GUILLEMIN

Maria Hanson
Leaf Bracelet, 1998
14 x 14 x 1 cm
Silver; hand fabricated, soldered, oxidized
PHOTO BY ARTIST

Kirsten Clausager

Untitled, 2003

3.5 x 9 x 9 cm

18-karat gold, sterling silver; cast, soldered, bent

PHOTO BY OLE AKHØJ

Julie A. Matheis

Repose Collection: Bracelet, 2003

10 x 10 x 5 cm
Feathers, thread; bound
PHOTO BY MARTY DOYLE
COURTESY OF SIENNA GALLERY,
LENOX, MASSACHUSETTS

I introduce materials into my work because of their inherent qualities and associative implications. Simultaneously strange yet familiar, they become physical and conceptual layers in a visual riddle. Intrinsic nuances are reinvented and sentiments transformed to evoke an intimate dialogue with open interpretations. Julie A. Matheis

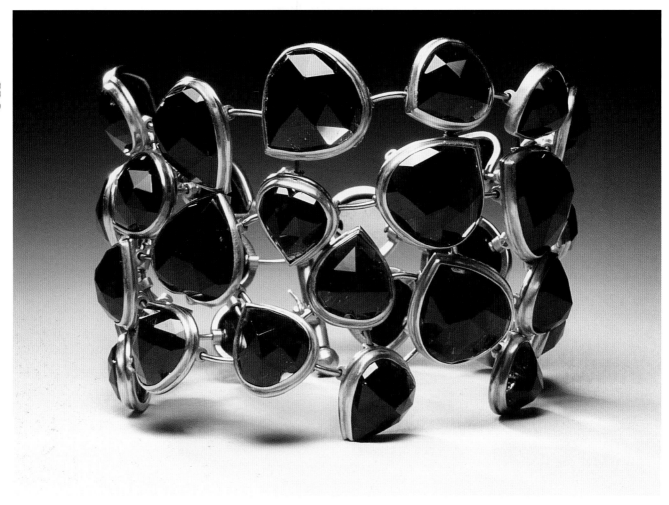

Lola Brooks
Bracelet, 2003

7.5 x 19 x 1 cm
Vintage rose-cut garnets, stainless steel, 18-karat gold;
hand fabricated, soldered, cast, hand faceted
PHOTO BY DEAN POWELL

Reiko Ishiyama
Untitled, 2002

10 x 13 x 5.5 cm
18-karat gold, sterling silver;
pierced, sandpaper finished,
riveted, oxidized
PHOTO BY RALPH GABRINER

When the starting point and the ending point are riveted together, what began as a flat sheet of sterling silver opens up into space. Reiko Ishiyama

Inês Nunes

Skin to Skin, 2002

Each, 12 x 10 x 11 cm
Pig intestine; engraved

PHOTOS BY FREDERICO AZEVEDO
AND CLAUDIO FERREIRA

Jan Wehrens
Untitled, 1987
11.5 x 32 x 10 cm
Steel
PHOTOS BY DIETMAR TANTERL

Tomoyo Hiraiwa
Do and *Sei (Motion* and *Calm)*, 2004

Each, 8 x 7 x 7 cm
Sterling silver; hammer formed, oxidized
PHOTO BY ARTIST

Anna Lindsay MacDonald
Perforated Möbius Strips 1, 2, 3, 2004
Each, 7 x 10 x 0.6 cm
Sterling silver; hand fabricated
PHOTO BY ARTIST

Each Möbius strip was perforated and pulled apart to reveal its new form. The action is demonstrated by the three phases of the strip.
Anna Lindsay MacDonald

Evan H. Larson

Acanthus, 2003

8.9 x 8.9 x 12.7 cm
Copper; fold formed
PHOTO BY ARTIST

Dongchun Lee

Untitled, 2004

Each, 2.4 x 7.2 cm in diameter
Sterling silver, iron; cast
PHOTO BY KWANG-CHOON PARK

Eric Larson
Taper, 2004

25.5 x 28 x 11.5 cm
Papier-mâché
PHOTO BY ARTIST

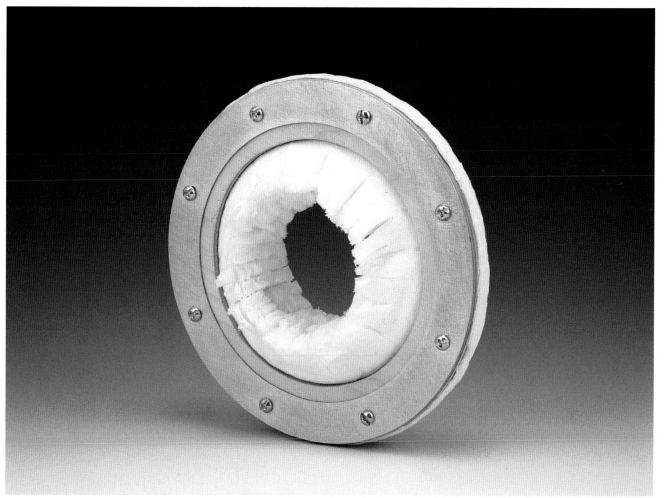

Gary J. Schott
Warning: Soft Material, 2004
12 x 12 x 4 cm
Aluminum, plywood, tissue, steel
nuts and bolts; hand fabricated
PHOTO BY ARTIST

Sandra Zilker
Big Donut Armlet, 2002

11.5 x 11.5 x 0.8 cm
Sterling silver, papier-mâché,
polymer clay, resin, pigments
PHOTO BY JACK B. ZILKER

Niyati Haft

Skin Bandage, 2004

6.5 x 18.5 x 6.2 cm
Leather, iron, smoky quartz, thread;
hand stitched, fabricated
PHOTO BY ARTIST

John Kent Garrott
Ice Bracelet, 2004
15.2 x 2.5 x 2.5 cm
Silver, ice
PHOTOS BY ARTIST

Christina Lin Ziegler
Untitled, 2002

8 x 10 x 3 cm
Sterling silver, walnut; hand fabricated, anticlastic raising
PHOTO BY CHRISTOPHER PACKER

Jacqueline Martell

Daphne Bracelet, 2004

35.6 x 12.7 x 12.7 cm
Wax, copper, wood, pigment, patina;
carved, electroformed, oxidized
PHOTO BY ADAM KRAUTH

Biba Schutz
Corsage Cuff, 2000

2.5 x 5 x 7.5 cm
Sterling silver, copper;
hand constructed, forged,
wrapped, oxidized
PHOTO BY RON BOSZKO

107

Stefano Marchetti

Untitled, 1997

8 x 8 x 7.5 cm

18-karat gold, sterling silver, shibuishi

PHOTO BY ROBERTO SORDI
COLLECTION OF MUSEÉ DES ARTS DÉCORATIFS,
PARIS, FRANCE

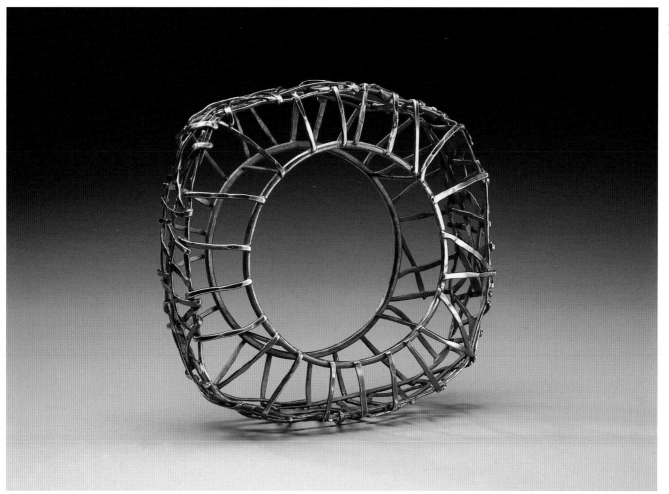

Alexandra Solowij Watkins-Janiye
Winter Hedge, 2003

10 x 3 cm
Silver; hand fabricated, swaged
PHOTO BY DEAN POWELL

Sharon Portelance

Wrist Corsage: Memory Breathes, 2003

7.6 x 3.8 x 2.5 cm
Sterling silver, 22-karat gold, 18-karat gold,
ribbon; hand fabricated
PHOTO BY ROBERT DIAMANTE

Seung Jin Lee

Traces, 2003

Left, 6 x 6 x 3.2 cm; right, 6.8 x 6.8 x 2.6 cm
Sterling silver; cast, fabricated, kum boo,
hollow constructed, oxidized

PHOTO BY KWANG-CHOON PARK

Giovanni Corvaja
Untitled, 2000
8.4 x 8.4 x 3.8 cm
18-karat gold; knitted
PHOTO BY ARTIST

Erik Urbschat

Unrund, 2000

Each, 7 x 6 x 1.8 cm
18-karat gold, sterling silver;
forged, assembled
PHOTO BY ARTIST

Elizabeth McDevitt

Untitled, 2003

6 x 5.5 x 5.5 cm

22-karat gold, 18-karat gold, black
jade, green jade, opal, tourmaline

PHOTOS BY KEITH ROBERTS

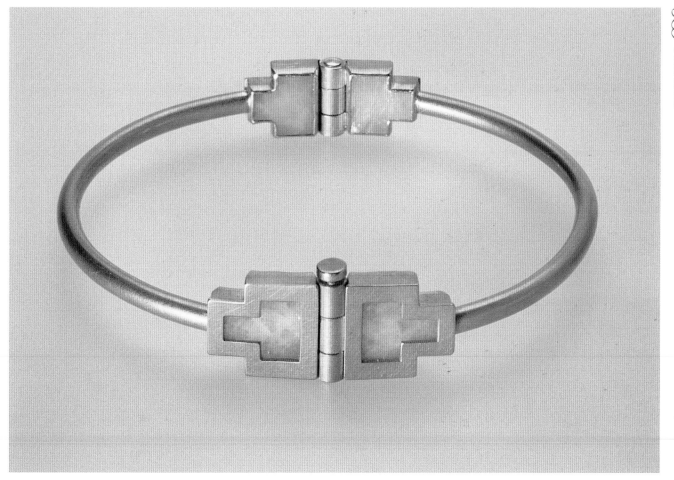

Christa Lühtje
Untitled, 1980

6.3 x 5.3 cm
22-karat gold, white jade
PHOTO BY EVA JÜNGER

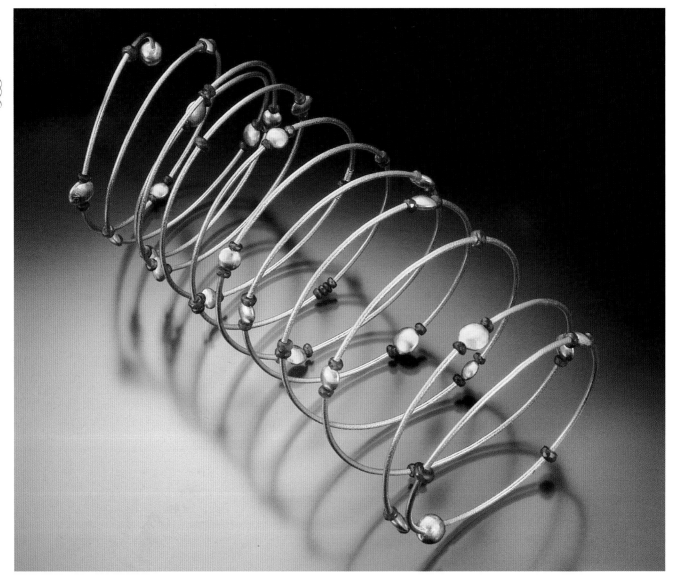

Gurhan

Spring Bracelet with Sapphires, 2000

19 cm

24-karat gold, sapphires

PHOTO BY RALPH GABRINER

Daniela Osterrieder
Wrap Around, 2001
Left, 3.5 x 6.5 x 5 cm; right, 5 x 6.5 x 5 cm
18-karat gold, sterling silver; hand fabricated
PHOTO BY ARTIST

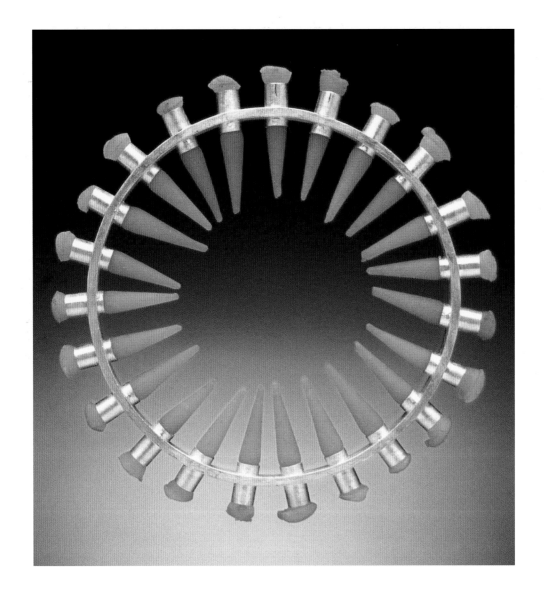

Sarah Doremus

Miller Analogy Bracelet Set A:
Soft is to Rubber What ___ is to Teeth, 2004

9.5 x 9.5 x 0.5 cm
Sterling silver, rubber; hand fabricated
PHOTO BY DEAN POWELL

Abrasha

"Royal" Pachinko Ball Bracelet, 1992

1.1 x 10.5 cm in diameter
Stainless steel, 18-karat gold, 24-karat gold,
steel pachinko balls

PHOTO BY RONNIE TSAI
COLLECTION OF OAKLAND MUSEUM OF CALIFORNIA,
OAKLAND, CALIFORNIA

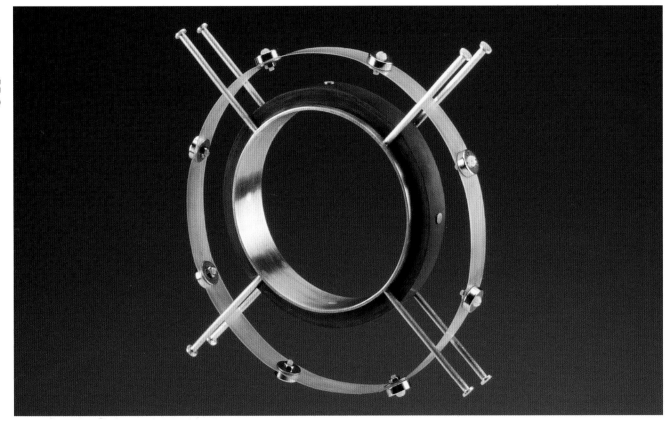

Erica Duffy

Magnetic Levitation Bracelet, 2003

17 x 17 x 2 cm
Sterling silver, nickel silver, stainless
steel, magnets, plastic; hand fabricated
PHOTO BY JEFF SABO

My interest lies in how things work—what does their structure look like, how are they put together, and what makes them go? This has led me to explore ways of creating movement, concentrating on the power of magnetism. The energy potential inside of a magnet is invisible. We can only see its power and its force through the reaction it creates with other materials. I explore these reactions and interactions in my work. **Erica Duffy**

David Damkoehler

Grosso Quadro (Bracelet with Two Bases), 1997
Bracelet, 9 x 10 x 2 cm; first base, 6 x 3 cm;
second base, 13 x 3 cm
Stainless steel; lathe turned, cold forged
PHOTO BY MICHAEL MAU
COLLECTION OF CHERYL GROSSO

Austenitic stainless steel—an alloy used in a wide range of objects including kitchen appliances, scientific instruments, and Rolex watches—is difficult to work, requiring special techniques and tools from the machine shop rather than the jewelry studio. One normally associates stainless steel with the utilitarian and scientific world, but I believe the metal is more interesting than other jewelry materials. It has a familiar burnished feeling that resonates indestructibility and purity to provide more distinctive metaphors.
David Damkoehler

Susie Ganch

Kinetic Bracelet #2, 2003

3 x 13 x 13 cm
Sterling silver, 18-karat yellow gold,
stainless steel, garnet; hand fabricated,
hollow constructed, forged, riveted,
oxidized
PHOTO BY PHILIP COHEN

Julia Turner

Monster Truck Series #2 and *#3*, 2001

Largest, 11 x 11 x 9 cm
Toy rubber truck tires, sterling silver; fabricated
PHOTO BY ARTIST

Reina Mia Brill
Eye Candy Bracelet #2, 2001

5 x 11.5 x 11.5 cm
Coated copper wire, silver-plated wire,
black onyx, magnets; hand knitted
PHOTO BY ARTIST

Gillian Munro
Kinetic Bangle, 2003
3 x 11 cm
Silver; oxidized
PHOTO BY ROGER '

**Takako
Muramatsu**
Untitled, 2004
11.4 x 11.4 cm
Fine silver, mohair,
sterling silver
PHOTO BY ARTIST

Alan Revere

Puzzle Bracelet, 1999

2 x 8.5 x 8.5 cm
Sterling silver, steel spring; fabricated
PHOTOS BY CHRISTINE DHEIN

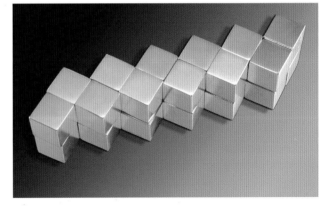

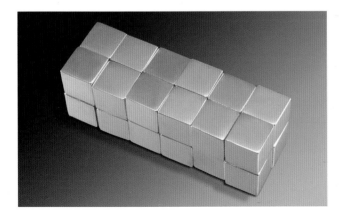

Hyeon-ju Noh
Night of the City, 2002
2 x 7 x 6.2 cm
Sterling silver
PHOTO BY MYUNG-WOOK HUH

Sarah McClary

Cactus Bracelet II, 2004

10 x 12 x 12 cm
Sterling silver; soldered, textured,
hinged, fold formed
PHOTO BY JOHN LUCUS

Dahlia Kanner
Cork Bracelet, 2002
17.5 x 2.5 x 0.2 cm
Sterling silver; cast, oxidized
PHOTO BY MARK JOHNSTON

Whitney L. Thompson

Organic Bracelet, 2004

9.5 x 11.5 x 6 cm
Sterling silver, aluminum
tubing, magnolia leaves;
hand fabricated, riveted
PHOTO BY JEFFREY SABO

Josée Desjardins

Lost at Sea II, 2004

4.8 x 15.9 x 14 cm

Found wood, cotton thread; hand fabricated

PHOTO BY ANTHONY MCLEAN
COURTESY OF GALERIE NOEL GUYOMARC'H,
MONTREAL, CANADA

Lost-and-found objects, especially those which have been tossed by the sea, challenge me. They carry a mysterious past. I like to partake in their journey and extend it through my work.
Josée Desjardins

SeungHee Clifton

Untitled, 2004

9.5 x 7 x 4.5 cm
Silver, frog closures; oxidized
PHOTO BY YUKO YAGISAWA

Inger Margrethe Larsen
My Precious Cuffs 2, 2002
Each, 8.5 x 8 x 7 cm
Textile, button, silver; sewn, electroformed
PHOTO BY ARTIST

133

Teresa Faris
Bracelet #1, 2004
3.8 x 14 cm in diameter
Latex
PHOTOS BY ARTIST

I am interested in jewelry as an extension of the body, similar to feathers on a bird. I chose Latex as the main material for this work because of its tactile qualities and its skin-like appearance. **Teresa Faris**

Carrie Perkins
Wax Bracelet, 2004
15.2 x 2.5 x 3.8 cm
Silver, beeswax, hydrangea blooms
PHOTO BY ARTIST

Cheri Overstreet

Maybe Next Spring, 2004

15.2 x 12.7 x 6.4 cm
Copper, crocus bulbs, allium bulbs, aluminum wire, hemp
rope, patina; hand fabricated, etched, formed, oxidized
PHOTO BY YUKO YAGISAWA

Eric Larson
Mussels, 2003
11.5 x 11.5 x 7.5 cm
Copper, synthetic diamonds
PHOTO BY ARTIST

Lynda Watson

Baja with the Guys, 2001

5 x 17 x 1.5 cm
Fine silver, sterling silver, pencil drawings on paper,
watch crystals, shells; hand fabricated, etched
PHOTO BY HAP SAKWA

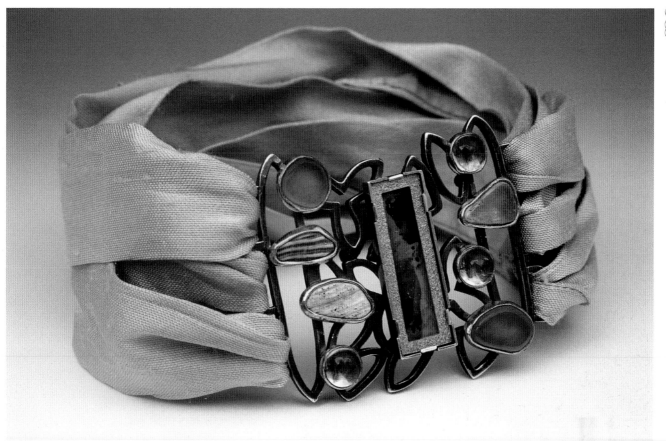

Loretta Fontaine

Eva on the Beach—Bishop's Lane Series, 2004

3.4 x 7.4 x 6.2 cm

22-karat gold, 14-karat gold, sterling silver, photographs, mica, aquamarines, beach glass, sea shells, barnacle, dupioni silk, patina; hand fabricated, granulation

PHOTO BY ARTIST
COURTESY OF TABOO STUDIO, SAN DIEGO, CALIFORNIA

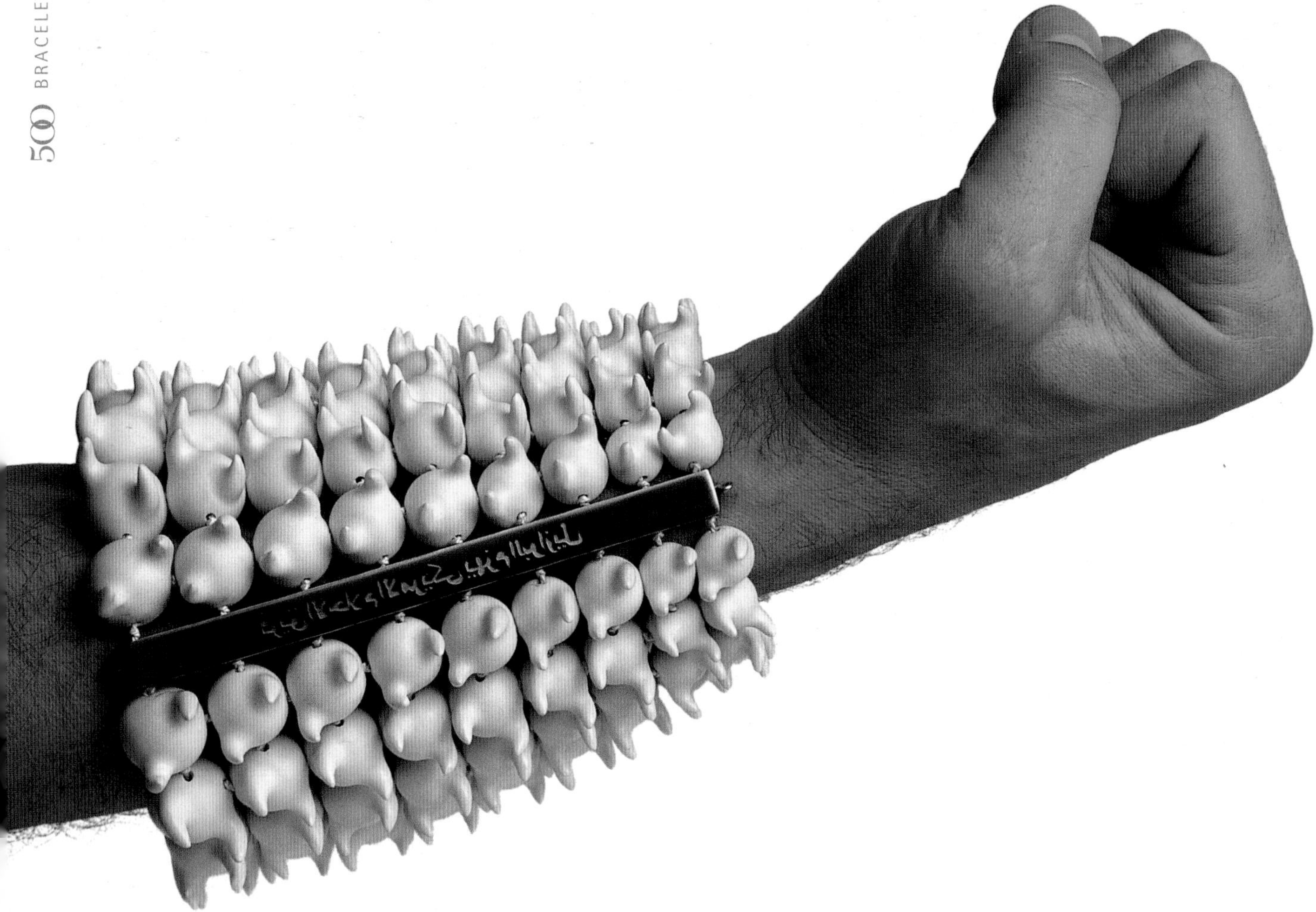

Peter Hoogeboom

Satanic Cuff, 1996

13.5 x 10 x 10 cm
Ceramic, silver, silk, alpaca
PHOTO BY HENNI VAN BEEK

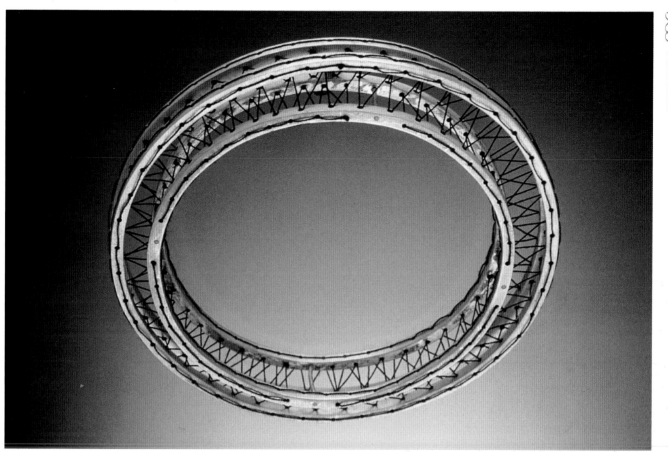

Patty L. Cokus

Tension–Compression Bracelet, 1998

8.6 x 8.6 x 1.2 cm
Sterling silver, thread, brass;
hand fabricated, drilled, sewn
PHOTO BY DEAN POWELL

Arthur David Hash

Hot-Glue Series Bracelet, 2004

16 x 16 x 10 cm
Hot glue, sterling silver; oxidized
PHOTO BY ARTIST

Joshua Salesin

Wave Bracelet, 2003

7.6 x 7.6 x 1.6 cm
African blackwood; hand turned
PHOTO BY ARTIST

Carolyn Bensinger

I Feel Pretty Bracelet, 2004

10.2 cm in diameter
Nylon fishing line, plastic sequins;
crocheted, sewn, flame heated
PHOTO BY DEAN POWELL

Salima Thakker

Modular Bracelet 1, 2002

4.5 x 20 x 0.7 cm
18-karat gold, sterling silver; hand fabricated
PHOTO BY PHOTOLOGY

Joining together numerous small,
wedge-shaped elements suggests
animal scales and spines. This piece
trails across and snakes around the
body. **Salima Thakker**

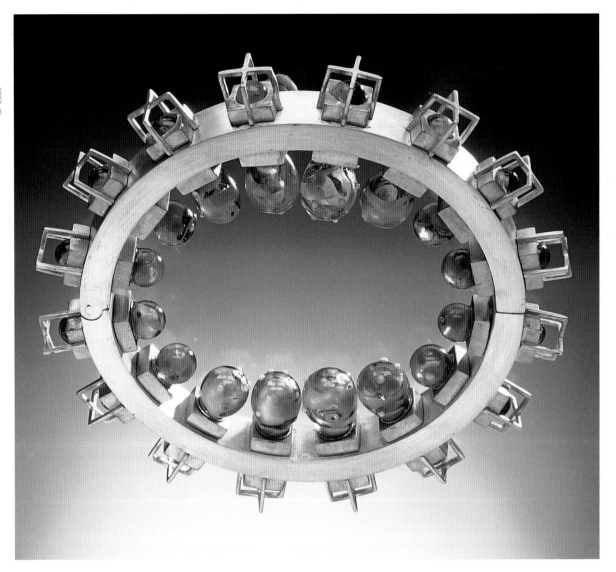

Lauren Kalman

Diffusion, 2002

8 x 8 x 1 cm
Sterling silver, 14-karat gold, glass; hollow
constructed, cast, lampworked, hinged
PHOTO BY DEAN POWELL

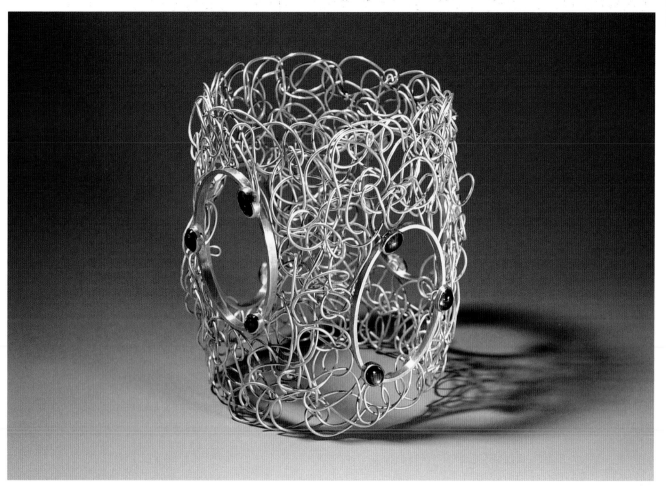

Anna Heindl

Pink Holes, 2001

9 x 6 x 0.5 cm
Sterling silver, red tourmalines
PHOTO BY MANFRED WAKOLBINGER

Kristy Pellicci
The Resolution, 2004

7.6 x 7 x 7 cm
Fine silver; hollow constructed, hand fabricated, etched
PHOTO BY LANELLE W. KEYS

Catherine Clark Gilbertson

Bending Toward the Sun, 2004

6 x 14 x 7 cm
Fine silver; chased, repoussé, formed
PHOTO BY HIROKO YAMADA

James Obermeier

The Only Space Left, 2003

15 x 15 x 2 cm
Sterling silver, 18-karat gold; hand fabricated, cast, hammered, oxidized
PHOTOS BY ARTIST

This body of work is concerned with the emergence of a new architectural landscape that has replaced the traditional ideals of natural beauty.
James Obermeier

Lanelle W. Keyes

Unfettered, 2002

15 x 7.5 x 2.5 cm
Iron, 23-karat gold leaf, paper;
forged, knotted
PHOTO BY DOUG YAPLE

Dana Driver

Channel Bracelet, 2001

8.8 x 11.3 x 1.3 cm
Sterling silver, basalt beach stones, fine
silver; anticlastic raising, carved, textured
PHOTO BY HAP SAKWA

Alessia Semeraro
Untitled, 2003

2 x 9 x 9 cm
Burnt cedar wood; fabricated
PHOTO BY ARTIST

Daniel Jocz

Aluminum Three Ways: Medusa, 2003

16.5 cm in diameter
Aluminum; carved, anodized
PHOTO BY DEAN POWELL

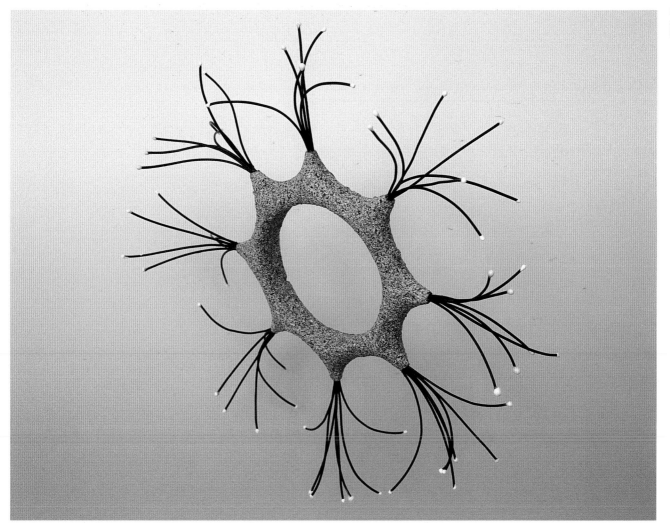

K.C. Calum
Untitled, 2004
23 x 23 x 3 cm
Wood, rubber, paint;
hand fabricated
PHOTO BY ARTIST

Kai Chan

Sunshine, White Sand Blue, 1984

7 x 34 x 30 cm and 7 x 34 x 28 cm
Palm leaf, acrylic paint, thread;
hand fabricated

PHOTO BY ARTIST
COURTESY OF GALERIE RA,
AMSTERDAM, NETHERLANDS

Kaori Taniguchi
Kawa, 2004

Each, 7 x 7 x 14 cm
Printed image, leather
PHOTO BY HIROYUKI ONO

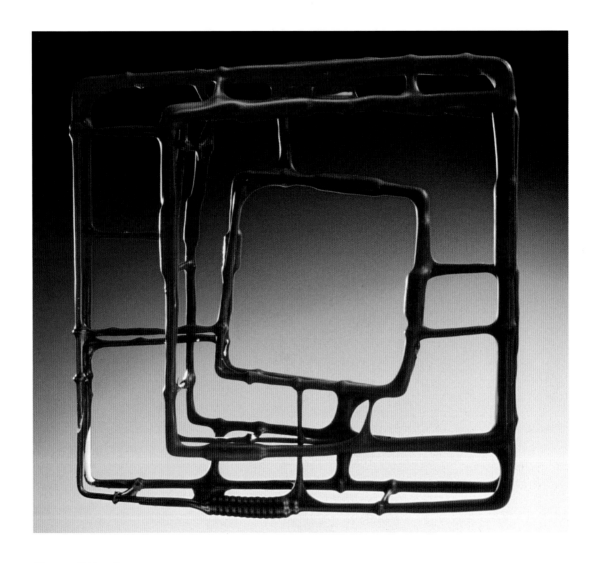

Donna D'Aquino

Wire Bracelet #59, 1999

14 x 14 x 39 cm
Steel, flexible rubber coating;
hand fabricated
PHOTO BY RALPH GABRINER

Ella Wolf

Untitled, 2003

5.5 x 2.5 x 4.5 cm

Glass beads, wire

PHOTO BY AMIRAM JABLONOVSKY

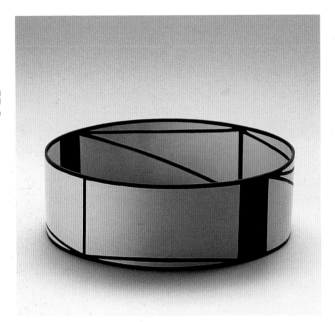
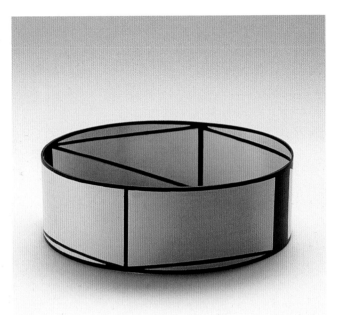

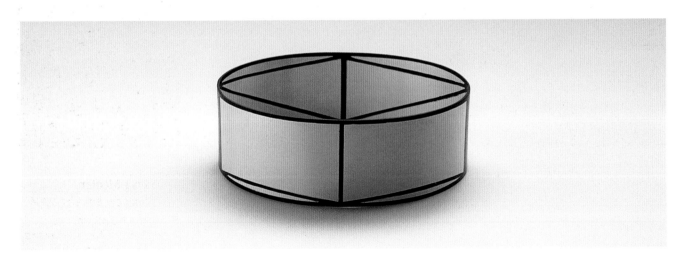

Shin-Lyoung Kim

Hidden Catch, 2004

2.5 x 8 cm in diameter
Sterling silver, nickel copper; married metal
PHOTOS BY ZAMIRO

Lisa Medlen

Shadow Bracelet, 2004

12 x 8.5 x 6 cm
Sterling silver, steel, patina;
hand fabricated, laser cut,
oxidized
PHOTO BY ARTIST

Jennifer Mokren

Duo, 2004

7.6 x 8.9 x 2.5 cm
Sterling silver, seed beads;
fabricated, peyote stitched
PHOTO BY ARTIST

Heejin Hwang

Heart, 2004

13 x 13 x 3.5 cm
Sterling silver, acrylic; hammered
PHOTO BY KWANG-CHOON PARK

163

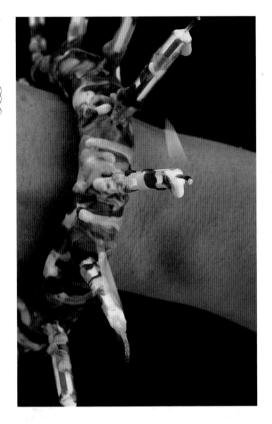

Angie Zent

Birthday, 2004

20.2 x 20.2 x 1.8 cm
Wax, birthday candles, crayons; formed, fabricated

PHOTOS BY JEFFREY SABO

Yeonkyung Kim
Bracelet, 2000
7 cm in diameter
Plastic
PHOTO BY ARTIST

Christel van der Laan

Priceless Bangle, 2004

24 x 24 x 4 cm
18-karat gold plate, sterling silver,
polypropylene swing tags; fabricated

PHOTOS BY ROBERT FRITH

Grethe Jilsøy
Snowflakes, 2003
1 x 11 x 2.5 cm
Acrylic; cut, filed, polished
PHOTO BY ARTIST

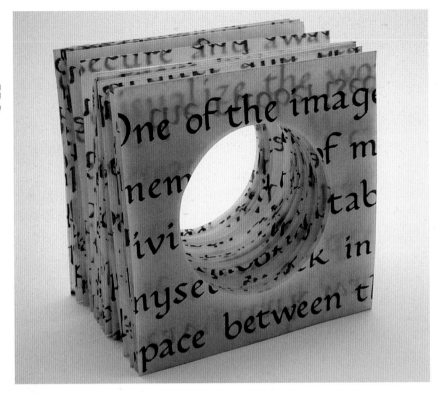

To make this accordion bangle, I produced calligraphic texts about my childhood on tissue paper. I manipulated the resulting material, folding, cutting the text, and playing with layers and transparency to create a fragile wearable in which memories are fragmented and partially displayed. **Francine Haywood**

Francine Haywood

Memories Bangle, 1999

10.2 x 10.2 x 0.5 cm
Calligraphy on tissue paper; folded, cut
PHOTOS BY ARTIST

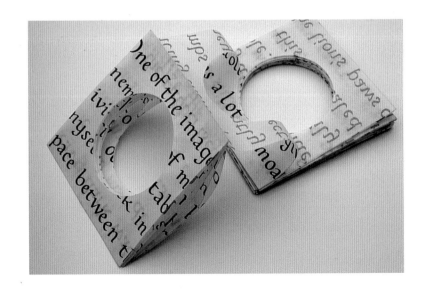

Ariane Hartmann
Motto Collection Bracelet, 2004
Each, 2 x 7 cm in diameter
Sterling silver; stamped, twisted
PHOTO BY ARTIST

Sigurd Bronger

Air Pressure, 1995

20 x 11 x 6 cm
Hard foam, lacquer, silver, rubber, steel, valve
PHOTO BY ARTIST
COLLECTION OF MUSEUM OF APPLIED ART, TRONDHEIM, NORWAY

Elisa Deval
Animal, 2004

78 cm long
Leather, 22-karat gold nails, silk thread,
millet seed; sawed, sewn, hammered
PHOTO BY BRUNO BRUCHI

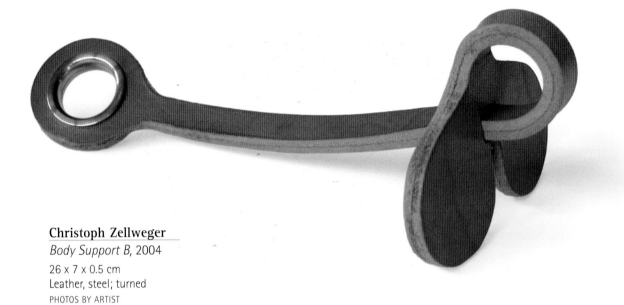

Christoph Zellweger
Body Support B, 2004
26 x 7 x 0.5 cm
Leather, steel; turned
PHOTOS BY ARTIST

Claude Schmitz

Ensemble, 2004

8 x 8 x 4 cm
Sterling silver, patina
PHOTO BY CHRISTIAN MOSAR

The five interlocking bangles
can be worn in different ways.
Claude Schmitz

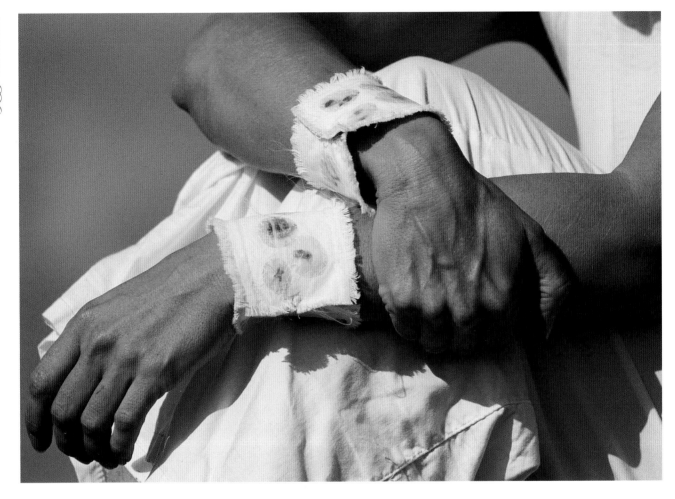

Åsa Halldin

Virus, 2004

Each, 7 x 6 cm in diameter
Cotton fabric, silk paper, wax, wool yarn, organza
PHOTO BY ADRIAN NORDENBORG

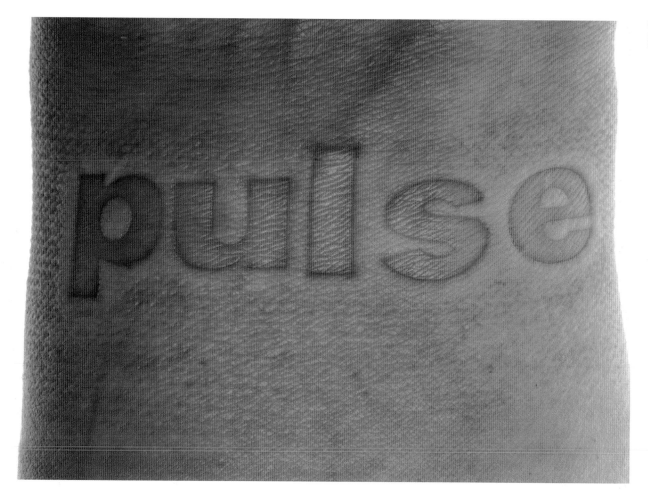

Tiffany Parbs
Etched, 2004

1.5 x 6 cm
Skin; imprinted
PHOTO BY GREG HARRIS

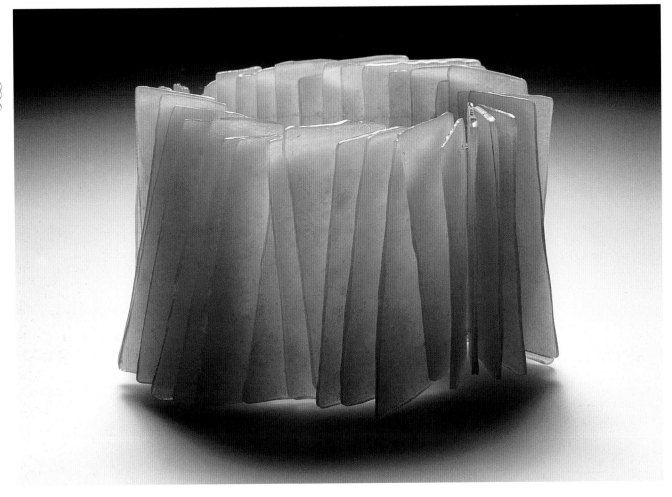

Yoko Shimizu

Untitled, 2004

6 x 8 cm in diameter
Rice paper, resin, nylon
PHOTO BY FEDERICO CAVICCHIOLI

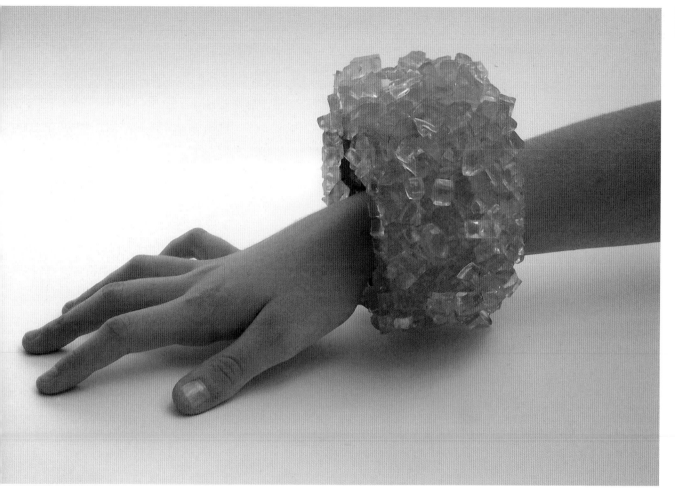

Roma Napoli and **Black Sifichi**

Bijoux Importable—Bracelet Made from Shattered Glass, 1997

14 cm in diameter
Shattered safety glass, plastic, silicone; hand fabricated
PHOTO BY FOTO SIFICHI

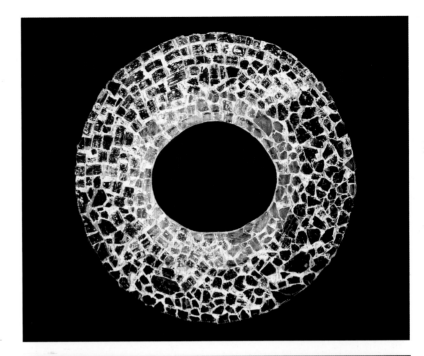

Robert W. Ebendorf

Bracelet, 2000

12.7 cm in diameter
Broken automotive glass, gesso, wood
PHOTOS BY BOBBY HANSSON

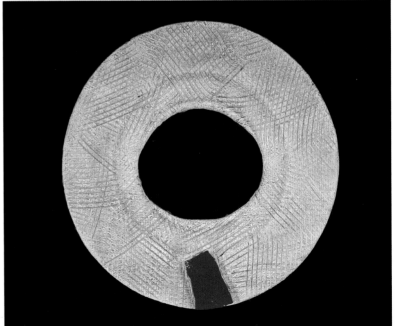

Kathy Buszkiewicz

Lining: The United States of America, 2004

7.4 x 11.4 x 11.4 cm
Sterling silver, U.S. currency, wood; hand fabricated,
engraved, lathe turned
PHOTOS BY ARTIST

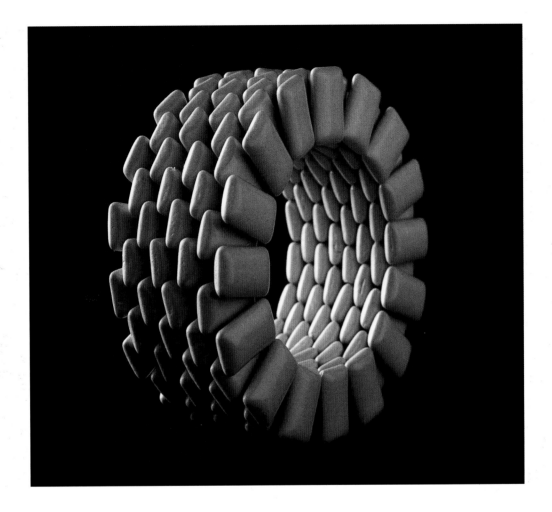

Ida Forss

Flashes of Taste, 2000

12 cm in diameter
Chewing gum; glued
PHOTO BY STEFAN KJÄLLSTIGEN

Mariana Sammartino

Hydrozoan, 2004

3.5 x 8 x 11 cm
Stainless steel mesh, sterling
silver; hand fabricated, ruffled,
layered, riveted
PHOTO BY ARTIST

Margaret McCombs

Cherry Blossom Bracelet, 2004

10 x 10 x 2.5 cm
Paper, monofilament
PHOTO BY ARTIST

Ella Wolf

An Embroidered Bracelet, 2002

8.5 x 1 x 5.7 cm
Yarn, embroidery thread
PHOTO BY AMIRAM JABLONOVSKY

Harriete Estel Berman

Column Bracelet, 2004

6.5 x 10.5 x 10.5 cm
Pre-printed steel from recycled containers,
plastic core; hand fabricated, pinked

PHOTO BY PHILIP COHEN

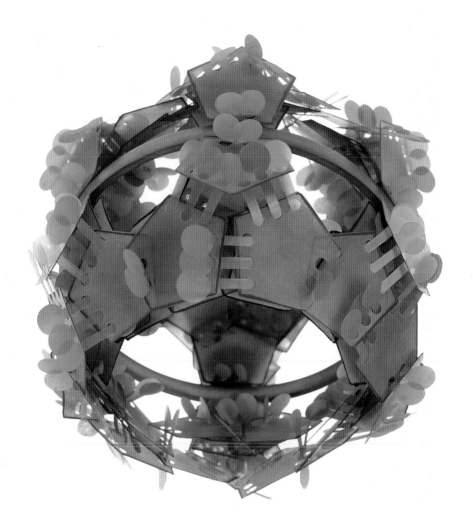

Svenja John

Vize, 2002

9 x 20 cm in diameter
Polycarbonate; hand fabricated, hand colored
PHOTO BY SILKE MAYER

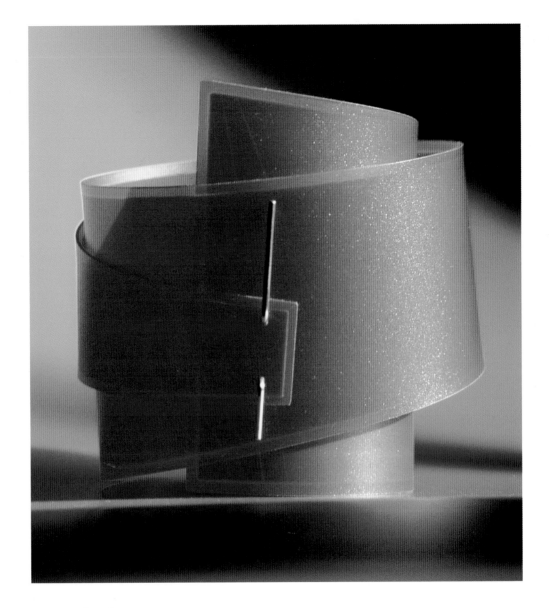

Gill Forsbrook
Untitled, 2001

8.5 x 9 x 9 cm
Polypropylene, polycarbonate, silver; hand fabricated
PHOTO BY ARTIST

Shannon Carney
Resin Bracelet #2, 2004
5 x 18 x 0.6 cm
Epoxy resin, sterling silver, monofilament
PHOTO BY ARTIST

Carol-lynn Swol

Spirograph Bracelet, Blue, 2004

11.4 x 10.8 x 7.6 cm
Tyvek, dye, sterling silver; cut, stacked, burned, soldered
PHOTO BY KEVIN MONTAGUE AND MICHAEL CAVANAGH

Julia M. Barello
Night Blossom Bracelet I, 2003
3.8 x 15.2 cm in diameter
X-ray film, MRI film, nylon; fabricated
PHOTO BY ARTIST

Felieke van der Leest

Rescue Ducklings in Pond
(Bracelet and Object), 2003

Bracelet, 5 x 20 x 20 cm
Yarns, felt, rubber, silver, 14-karat
gold, topaz, purchased toys;
crocheted, fabricated

PHOTO BY EDDO HARTMANN
COLLECTION OF THE DUTCH TEXTILE
MUSEUM, TILBURG, NETHERLANDS

Tina Tvedt
Life Buoy for an Arm 2, 2004
4 x 11 x 11 cm
Polyester, aluminum, light-emitting diodes; sewn
PHOTO BY STEN MAGNE KLANN

Ella Wolf

I Am the House, I Am the Tree, I Am the Jewel, 2002

Left, 17 x 10 x 10 cm; right, 30 x 13 x 13 cm
Yarn, fabric, embroidery thread
PHOTO BY AMIRAM JABLONOVSKY

Hyun Shin

Untitled, 2004

10.2 x 5 x 5 cm
Paper, papier-mâché

Jennifer L. Sholtis

Spiral Brace III, 2003

15.2 x 14 x 3.2 cm
Epoxy resin, nylon;
CAD/CAM rapid proto-
typed, stereolithography,
selective laser sintered
PHOTO BY ARTIST

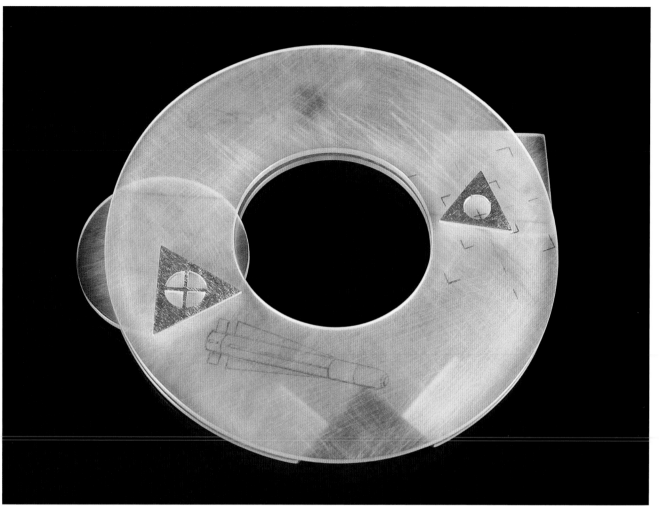

Karen McCreary
Infinite Threat, 2001

15.5 x 16 x 1 cm
Acrylic, aluminum, lacquer,
pencil, drawing; hand fabricated, riveted
PHOTO BY ARTIST

Nikky Bergman
Flagella Bracelet (detail), 2004

Cuff, 12.7 x 5.1 cm; longest flagellum, 91.4 cm
Fine silver, plastic, pigment; fabricated,
heat shaped
PHOTO BY ADAM KRAUTH

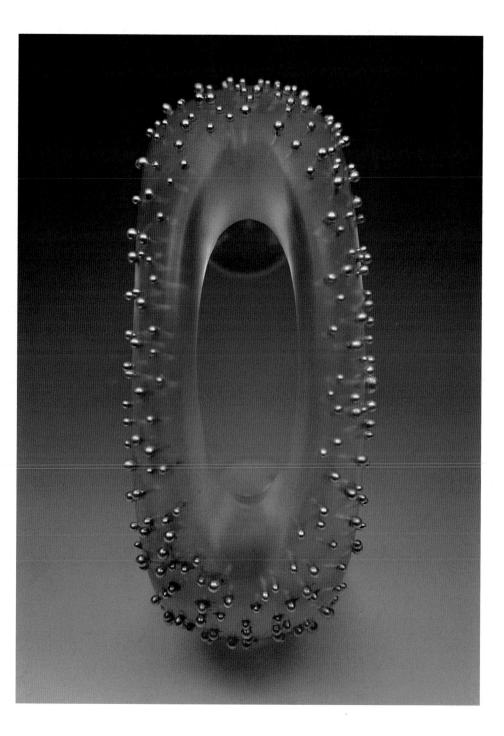

Chris Irick
Untitled, 2003

4 x 8 x 7 cm
Acrylic, fine silver; hand
fabricated, carved, sanded,
sandblasted, heat shaped
PHOTO BY ARTIST

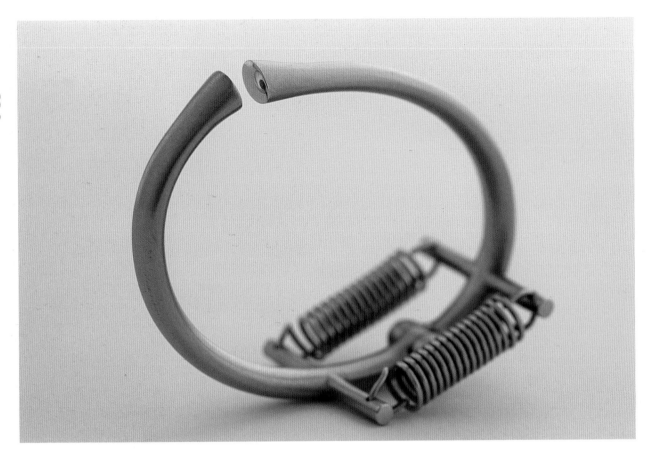

Sean O'Connell

Snap Trap Bracelet, 2002

6.5 x 7.5 x 4 cm
Stainless steel, 9-karat white gold; forged,
lathe turned, TIG welded

PHOTOS BY ALBERT PACA

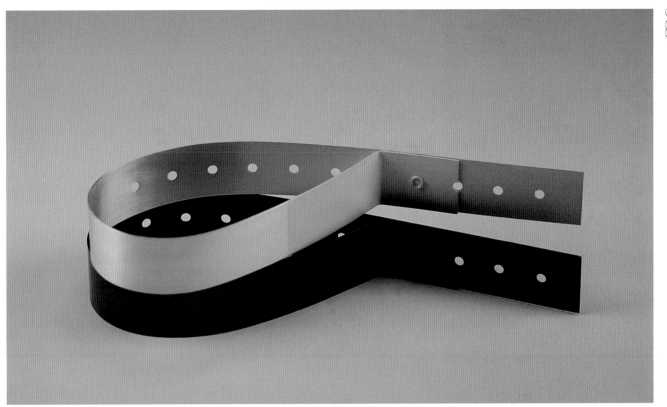

Christie Laingor
I.D., 2003
Each, 2 x 18.2 x 7.8 cm
Sterling silver; hand fabricated, oxidized
PHOTO BY JEFF SABO

Deniz Tirpanci

Untitled, 2004

4 x 1.5 x 9 cm in diameter
Copper, brass, beads, nail enamel, patina;
hand raised, hand painted

PHOTO BY TAYLOR DABNEY

Peg Fetter

Joan's Bracelet, 2002

5 x 8 x 2.5 cm
Steel, 14-karat gold, uncut
industrial diamond; forged,
soldered, heat beaded, fabricated,
bezel set, heat oxidized, waxed
PHOTO BY DON CASPER
PRIVATE COLLECTION

Lola Brooks

Two Bracelets, 2002

2 x 2 x 18 cm
Stainless steel, vintage rose-cut
garnets, 18-karat gold; hollow
constructed, soldered

PHOTO BY DEAN POWELL

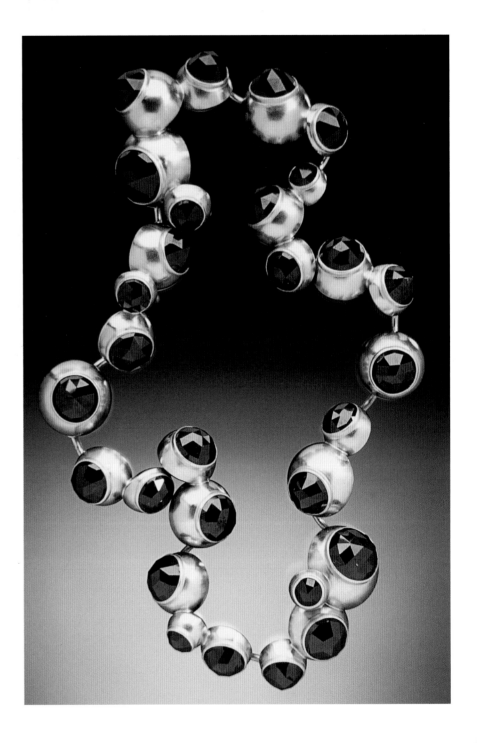

Daniel Kruger
Untitled, 1996

12.5 x 7.5 cm
18-karat gold, Nepalese stained amber,
aquamarine, rubelite, green garnet,
orange garnet, pearl; hand fabricated
PHOTO BY THILO HAERDTLEIN
PRIVATE COLLECTION

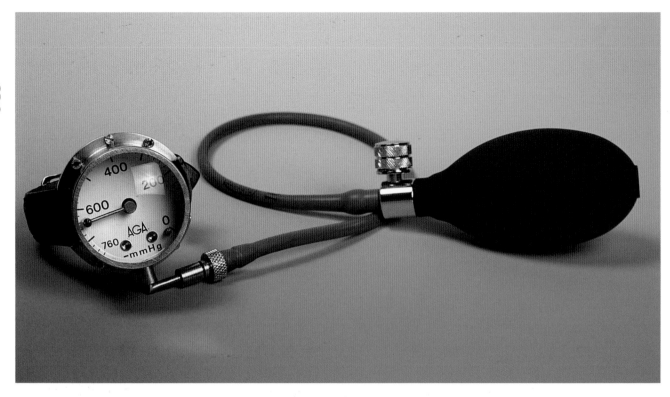

Sigurd Bronger
Hand Shake Meter, 2002

3 x 1.5 cm
Fine gold, brass, lens, rubber, leather
PHOTO BY ARTIST

McIrvin Field-Sloan

Pours, 2003

6.5 x 12.5 x 2.5 cm
Sterling silver, glass, gold leaf, water, detergent,
epoxy; hand fabricated, blown
PHOTO BY ROBERT DIAMANTE

Mecky van den Brink
dog's faith, 1994
16 x 14 x 6 cm
Gold, porcelain
PHOTO BY HENNIE VAN BEEK

Yuki Murata

Whiteware 001, 2004

Left, 5 x 7.5 x 0.4 cm; center, 4.2 x 7.5 x 0.4 cm; right, 3.5 x 7.5 x 0.4 cm
Porcelain; slip cast, painted
PHOTO BY ARTIST

Harriete Estel Berman

*Bead Embellishment
Bracelets,* 2004

Largest, 17.8 cm
Pre-printed steel from recycled
containers, plastic core; hand
fabricated, pinked, hydraulic
press formed
PHOTO BY PHILIP COHEN

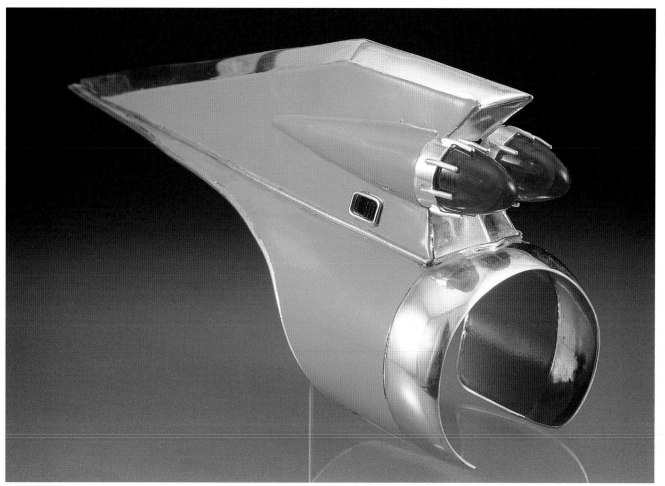

Amy K. Conrad
'59 Caddy Tail Fin Bracelet, 2003

7.6 x 5 x 15.2 cm
Sterling silver, copper, urethane paint, electronics;
hand fabricated, hollow constructed
PHOTO BY ROB JACKSON

Anna Heindl

Sunset, 2001

7 x 6 x 2 cm
18-karat gold, silver, citrines,
carnelian, sunstones; oxidized
PHOTO BY MANFRED WAKOLBINGER

Otto Künzli

Gold Makes Blind, 1980

Variable dimensions; gold sphere, 1.2 cm in diameter
Rubber, gold
PHOTO BY ARTIST

Christoph Zellweger
Body Support B, 2004

20 x 6.5 x 0.5 cm
Leather, steel; turned
PHOTOS BY ARTIST

Todd Turner

Lifeforms Bracelets: Motherchild, Seed, Organic, 2003

Each, 6.5 x 5.5 x 3 cm
Sterling silver, moonstone; hand fabricated
PHOTO BY ARTIST

Eun Mi Kim

Different Thoughts, 2002

6.7 x 6.7 x 1.5 cm
Sterling silver, stainless steel balls,
gold; hand fabricated, hinged,
gilded, riveted, box catch
PHOTO BY MYUNG UK HEO

Each unit turns by built-in balls and shows both
positive and negative figures. **Eun Mi Kim**

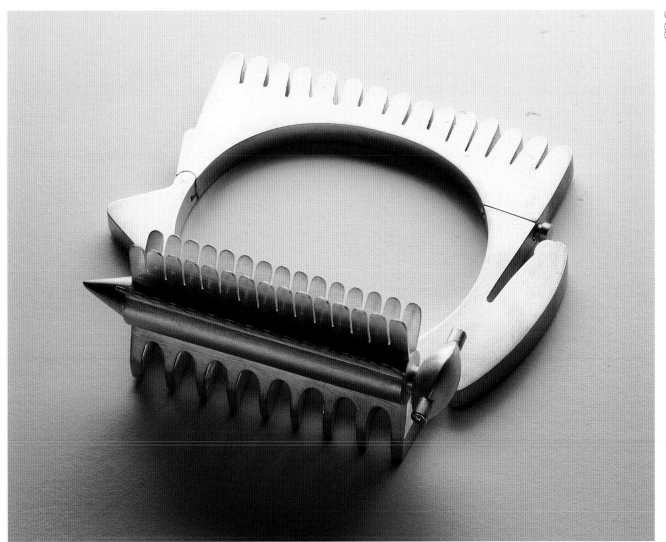

Barbara Paganin
Pterigota, 1993
2 x 7.5 x 6.5 cm
18-karat gold, diamonds; hand fabricated
PHOTO BY LORENZO TRENTO

Ronda Coryell
Untitled, 2001

2 x 9 x 7 cm
22-karat gold, sterling silver,
blue sapphire cabochons; hand
fabricated, riveted, granulation

PHOTO BY GEORGE POST

Incorporating something traditional and ancient, and making it modern yet regal is the focus of my work. The process of granulation is an exciting experience. It must be pushed to the limits—worked on the edge between success and failure. **Ronda Coryell**

Caroline V. Steinau-Steinrück
Untitled, 2004

7.5 cm in diameter
20-karat gold, thermoplastic
PHOTO BY EVA JÜNGER

Chih-Wen Chiu

Terrifying Waves, 2002

12.7 x 9.5 x 10.2 cm
Fine silver; hand fabricated,
hammered, folded
PHOTO BY DAN NEUBERGER

Dorothée Rosen

One Year Bracelet, 2004

8 cm in diameter
Sterling silver; forged, constructed
PHOTO BY ARTIST

Flora Book
Abacus Cuff, 2002
7.5 x 7.5 x 7.5 cm
Sterling silver; woven
PHOTO BY ROGER SCHREIBER

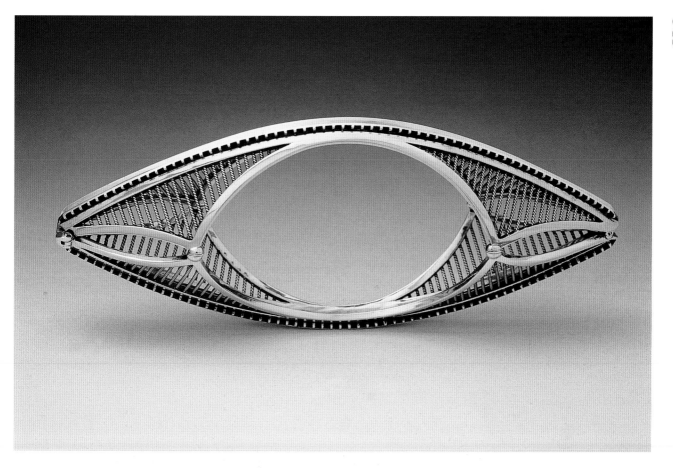

Sergey Jivetin

Bridge Bracelet, 1999

6 x 12 x 2 cm
Sterling silver; hand fabricated
PHOTO BY ARTIST
COLLECTION OF LISA M. BERMAN

I wanted to surround the wrist with a light, open, and perfectly balanced structure that would highlight and define the geometry of the hand and its gestures. **Sergey Jivetin**

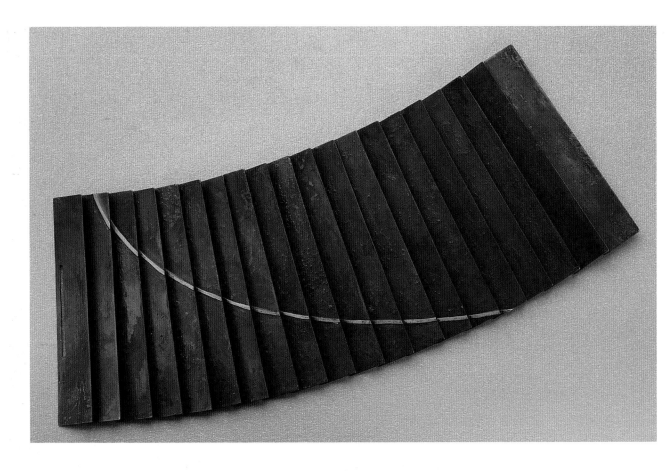

Yoko Shimizu
Untitled, 2004

7.5 x 20 cm
Silver, 24-karat gold, 18-karat gold; niello
PHOTOS BY FEDERICO CAVICCHIOLI

Reiko Ishiyama
Untitled, 2000

6 x 9 x 9.5 cm
14-karat gold, sterling silver; hammered,
textured, pierced, riveted, oxidized
PHOTO BY RALPH GABRINER

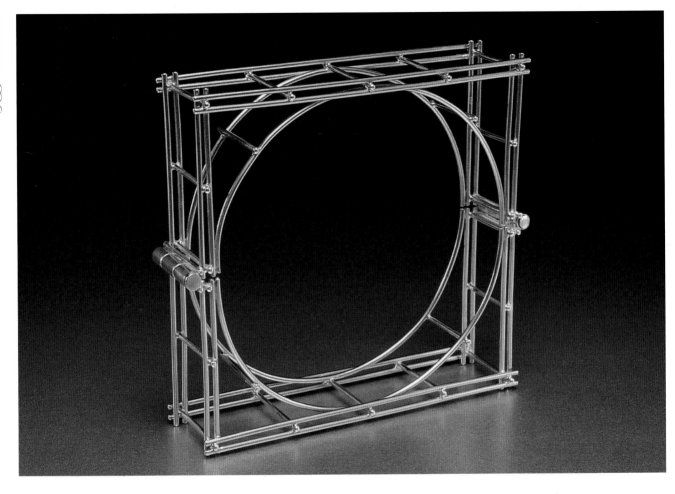

Ben Neubauer

Untitled, 2004

6 x 6.5 x 2 cm

Sterling silver, 18-karat gold; fabricated

PHOTO BY COURTNEY FRISSE
COURTESY OF FACÈRÈ JEWELRY ART GALLERY,
SEATTLE, WASHINGTON

Like the skeleton of a building, my work is constructed to be both light and strong.

Ben Neubauer

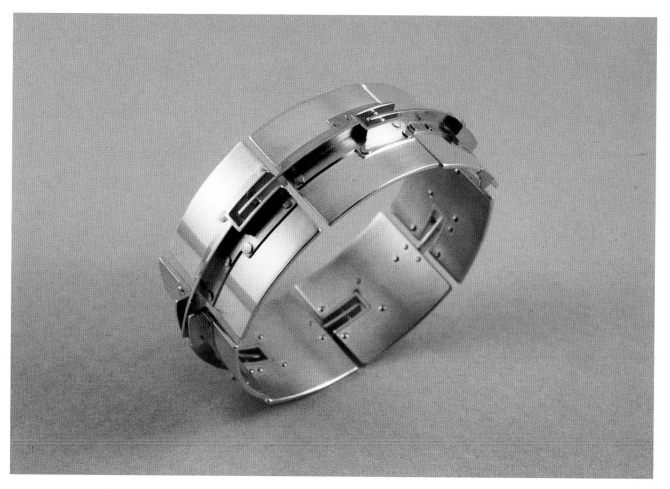

Abrasha

Untitled, 1986

17 x 2.2 x 0.5 cm
Sterling silver, 18-karat gold, 24-karat gold;
hand fabricated, riveted
PHOTO BY ARTIST

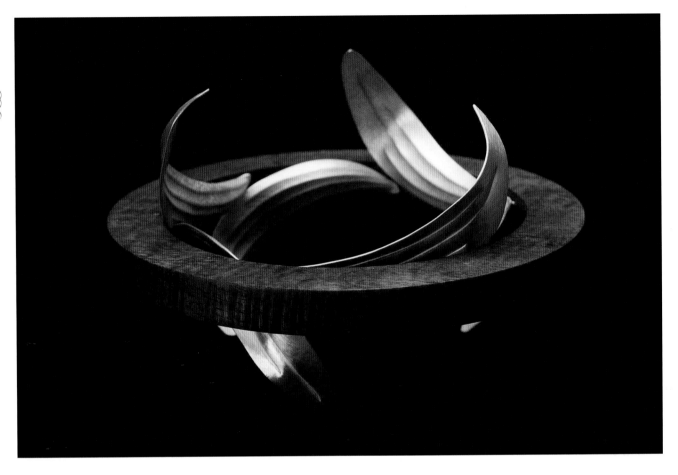

Dayna Mae Orione

Koa, 2004

11.5 x 11.5 x 6.5
Silver, koa wood; matting,
chased, repoussé, hand carved, lined
PHOTO BY ALAN FARKAS

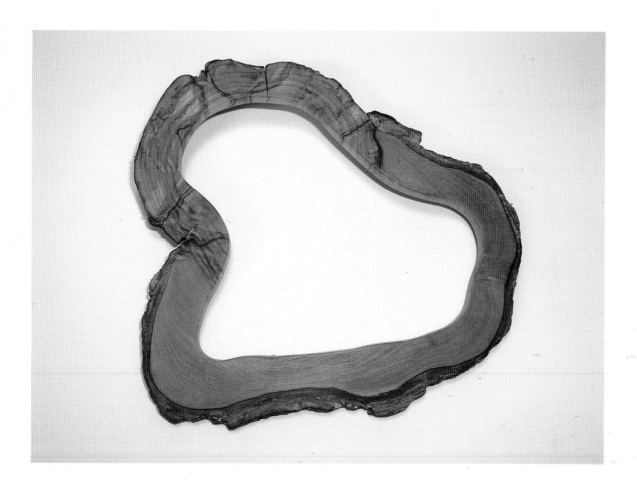

Silje Bergsvik
Untitled, 2004
9.9 x 11.3 x 0.6 cm
Wood; hand fabricated
PHOTO BY SHANNON CARNEY

Philip J. Hoffman

Skins, 2003

5 x 8 x 6 cm
Rubber, plastic, oil paint; hand fabricated
PHOTO BY NORMAN WATKINS

Deborah Lozier

Welded Study in Stripes, 1998

9 x 9 x 2 cm
Enamel, copper; fold formed, anticlastic
raising, welded, torch fired

PHOTO BY ERIC SMITH

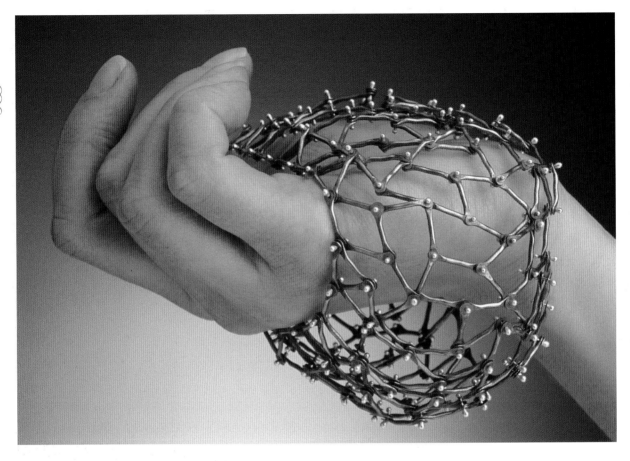

Kristine J. Bolhuis

Mesh System Bracelet—Pentagonal, 2002

8.3 x 8.9 x 8.9 cm
Nickel, sterling silver; forged, hand fabricated, riveted
PHOTO BY JOHN GUILLEMIN

In an exciting process of exploration and discovery, I constantly manipulate my material, never knowing exactly what the final outcome will be, always keeping an open mind about the possibilities along the way. This process is evident in the work. The bracelets have inherent mobility and mutability, which encourages the wearer to manipulate their parts. Through handling, the jewelry reveals its essential structures and geometric patterns to the wearer.
Kristine J. Bolhuis

Kathy Buszkiewicz

Lining: Series, 2003

2.2 x 12.2 x 12.2
Sterling silver, U.S. currency, wood;
hand fabricated, lathe turned
PHOTOS BY ARTIST

Nicky Falkenhayn

Tendinitis, 2004

Unrolled, 152.4 x 3.2 x 0.2 cm
Fine silver, 14-karat gold; knitted, oxidized

PHOTO BY ARTIST
COURTESY OF GARI FINE JEWELRY & HOME ACCENTS,
PORTLAND, OREGON

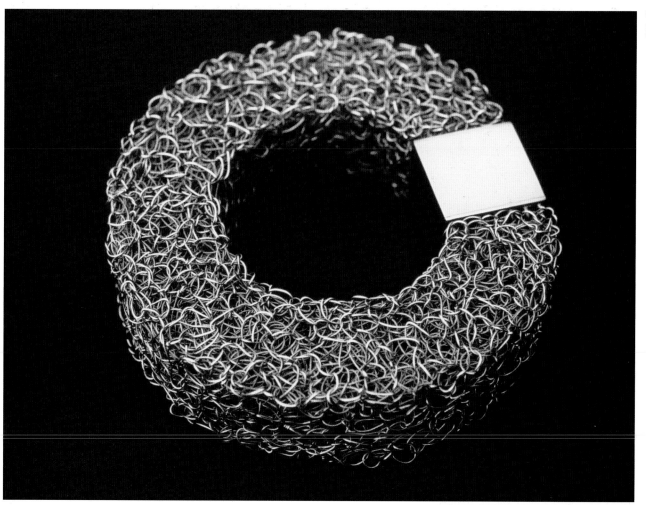

Petra Schou
Cube, 1998
3 x 12 x 12 cm
Silver; oxidized
PHOTO BY ARTIST

Shona Rae

The Three Muses, 2004

14 x 10 x 8 cm
Copper screen, acrylic paint;
hand sculpted, hand formed
PHOTO BY ARTIST

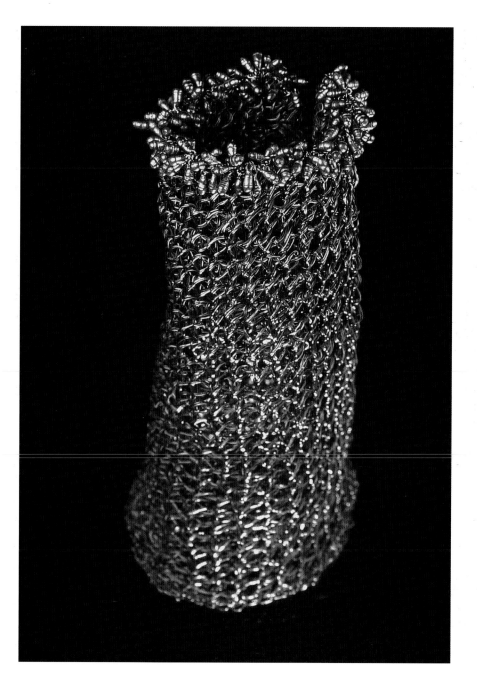

Inger Blix Kvammen

Silver and Copper Crochet with Silver Pearls, 2004

20 x 23 cm
Sterling silver, coated copper; oxidized, hand fabricated, crocheted
PHOTO BY LENE STAVÅ JENSEN

Nina Basharova

Milky Way & *Black Hole*, 2004

6 x 8 x 6 cm
Sterling silver; fabricated, cast, soldered
PHOTO BY BRYAN MCCAY

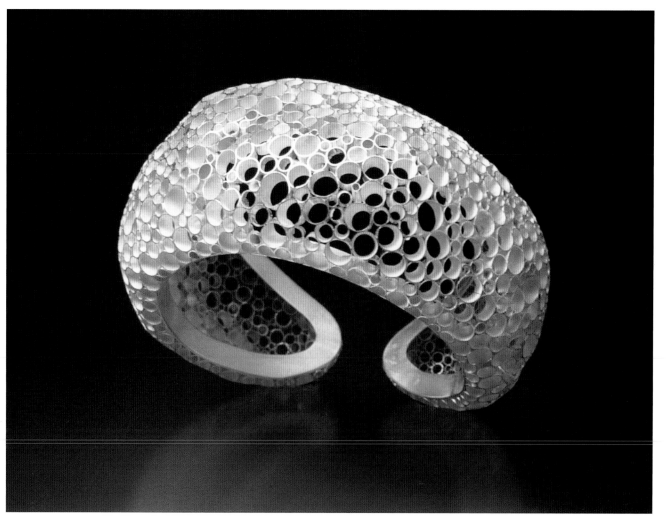

Anya Pinchuk
Untitled, 2003

5 x 6 x 2 cm
Sterling silver; hand fabricated
PHOTO BY ARTIST

Dayna Mae Orione

Untitled, 2001

24 x 22 x 2.2 cm
Silver, feathers; hand fabricated,
friction-fit clasp
PHOTO BY ALAN FARKAS

Brigit Daamen
Multiple, 2003
Each, 3.5 x 10 x 10 cm
Wool; hand felted
PHOTOS BY ARTIST

Multiple begins as one piece and is cut to become a set of six individual bracelets. The cutting is meant as a ritual that emphasizes the bond between the people involved—friends or family. **Brigit Daamen**

Marjorie Schick

Spinning Wheels Pair of Armlets
(one of a pair), 2001

14 x 16.5 cm in diameter
Wood, paint; constructed
PHOTO BY GARY POLLMILLER

Kim da Sul
Amaging, 2003
12 x 15 x 15 cm
Plastic, gold leaf, rabbit fur
PHOTO BY PRISM

Kristy Modarelli
Untitled, 2004

3 x 10 x 3 cm
Polymer clay, cubic zirconia;
hand sculpted, hand polished
PHOTO BY ARTIST

This bracelet is about tactile beauty as much as it is about visual beauty. **Kristy Modarelli**

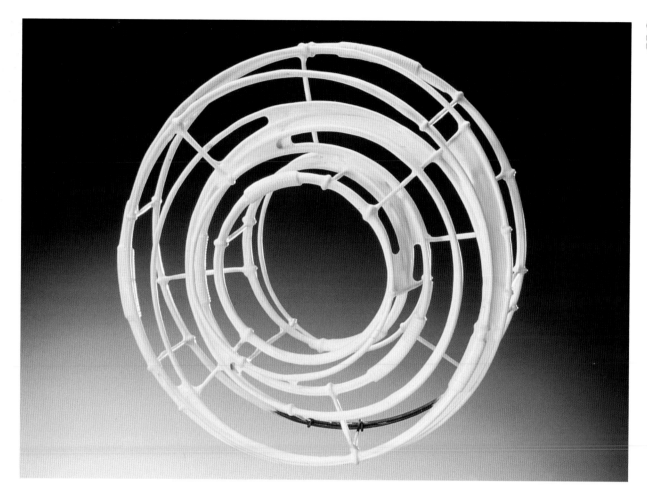

Donna D'Aquino
Wire Bracelet #91, 2004
16.5 x 16.5 x 9 cm
Steel, flexible rubber coating;
hand fabricated
PHOTO BY RALPH GABRINER

Christine Marie Noguere

Aphrodite 3000, 2003

8.3 x 6.4 x 5.1 cm
Japanese glass cylinder seed beads,
freshwater pearls, wooden bead, rubber
ring, brass blank, Ultrasuede; off-loom
bead weaving using peyote stitch and
right angle weave, sewn
PHOTO BY PHIL POPE

This piece is inspired by the myth surrounding the
goddess Aphrodite's birth at sea. As drops of water
dripped off her body, they changed into pearls and fell
into the ocean. **Christine Marie Noguere**

Inger Blix Kvammen
Silvernest with Blue Pearls, 2003

7 x 19 cm
Sterling silver, freshwater pearls; oxidized,
hand fabricated, crocheted
PHOTO BY BÅRD STIEN

Sharon Portelance

Wrist Corsage: Ever Present, 2003

7.6 x 3.8 x 3.2 cm
Sterling silver, 18-karat gold, 22-karat gold,
ribbon; hand fabricated
PHOTO BY ROBERT DIAMANTE

Billie Jean Theide
Black Ruin, 2003

8.3 cm in diameter
Sterling silver; cast, fabricated,
oxidized
PHOTO BY ARTIST

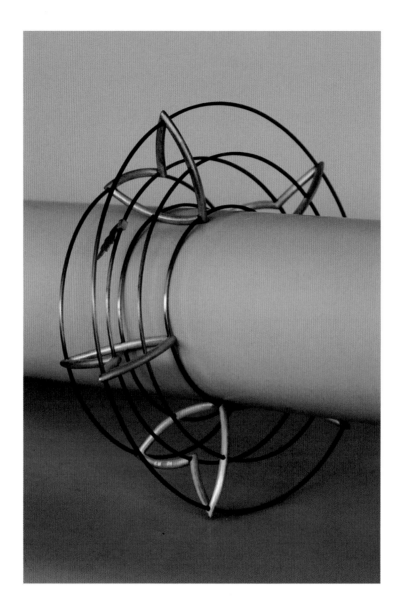

Carlier Makigawa

Untitled, 1995

13.5 x 13.5 x 4.5 cm
Sterling silver, nickel-copper alloy,
18-karat gold; hand fabricated
PHOTO BY ARTIST

Claude Schmitz

Chicago, 2004

9 x 9 x 3 cm
Sterling silver, patina
PHOTO BY CHRISTIAN MOSAR

Mizuko Yamada

Tactile Bracelet, 2004

9.5 x 7.5 x 11.5 cm
Copper, silver; hammered, plated
PHOTOS BY ARTIST

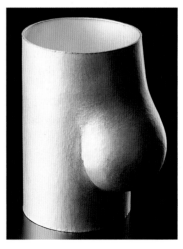

Monica Schmid

Sculpture Bracelet, 2004

11 x 8 x 9 cm
Sterling silver; forged, hollow
construction, fabricated
PHOTO BY PHILIP COHEN

Forging metal may seem laborious and
time consuming, but for me it's a medi-
tative process, a way to connect with the
material and the shape I'm creating.
Although I start out with a general plan,
I never let my initial intentions get in the
way of exploring new shapes. I abandon
the initial idea when the metal acquires
its own language. **Monica Schmid**

Margareth Sandström
Untitled, 1989

4 x 7 x 6 cm
Silver; hand fabricated
PHOTO BY SUNE SUNDAHL

Babette von Dohnanyi
Crystal Bracelet, 2004

3.7 x 6 cm
Sterling silver; soldered, cast
PHOTO BY FEDERICO CAVICCHIOLI

Lynda Watson

Alan and Gypsy's Ireland, 2001

6.5 x 18 x 2.5 cm
Sterling silver, 24-karat gold foil,
pencil drawings on paper,
watch crystals, stones, shells;
hand fabricated, etched, oxidized
PHOTO BY HAP SAKWA

Melanie Seiler
Untitled, 2004

5 x 5 x 5 cm
Sterling silver, small light source,
silk; wax cast
PHOTO BY ARTIST

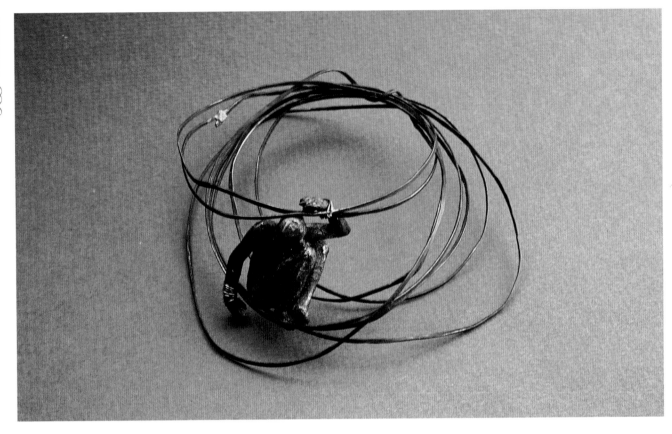

Monica Guevara

A Dream, 2003

9 cm in diameter
Sterling silver, 18-karat gold;
cast, hand fabricated, oxidized
PHOTO BY ARTIST

I try to let my hands work with as little interference as possible from the rational part of my mind, so as to express sensations and emotions that belong to me as an individual, and to us all as human beings. Monica Guevara

Masumi Kataoka
Untitled, 2004

10 x 2 x 10 cm
24-karat gold, human hair;
knotted, soldered
PHOTO BY ARTIST

Svenja John

Priel, 2002

8 x 10 cm in diameter
Polycarbonate; surface treated,
hand colored, hand fabricated
PHOTO BY SILKE MAYER

Jennifer Ramirez
Untitled, 2004

8.9 x 15.2 x 15.2 cm
Paper, aluminum mesh, fabric flower parts,
embroidery thread
PHOTO BY NATALYA PINCHUK

Barbara Stutman

Royal Cuff, 2004

6.3 x 8.9 x 10.8 cm
Fine silver, copper, silver plate,
copper wire, vinyl lacing, glass
seed beads; crocheted

PHOTO BY ANTHONY MCLEAN
COURTESY OF GALERIE NOEL
GUYOMARC'H, MONTREAL, CANADA

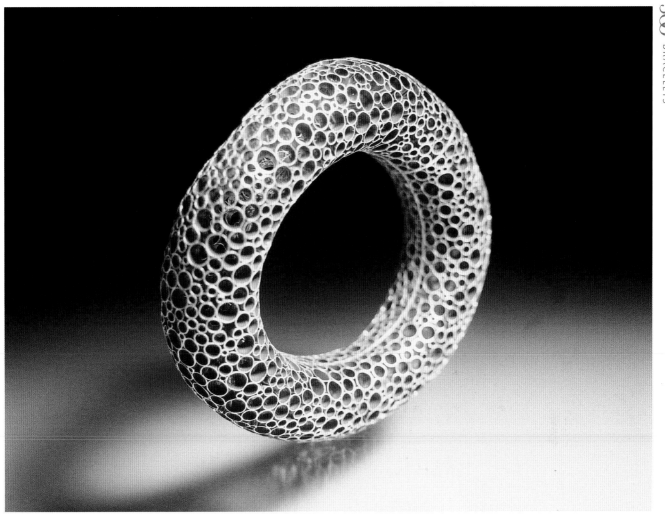

Anya Pinchuk
Untitled, 2004

5 x 5 x 1 cm
Sterling silver, paint; hand fabricated
PHOTO BY ARTIST

Ting-Ting Tsao

MEMO II, 2004

15 x 6 x 3.5 cm
Self-adhesive notes; written, hand fabricated
PHOTO BY KAREN LUNG TSAI

Carol-lynn Swol
Spirograph Bracelet, Red, 2004
12.7 x 10.8 x 5.7 cm
Tyvek, dye, sterling silver; cut,
stacked, burned, soldered
PHOTO BY KEVIN MONTAGUE AND
MICHAEL CAVANAGH

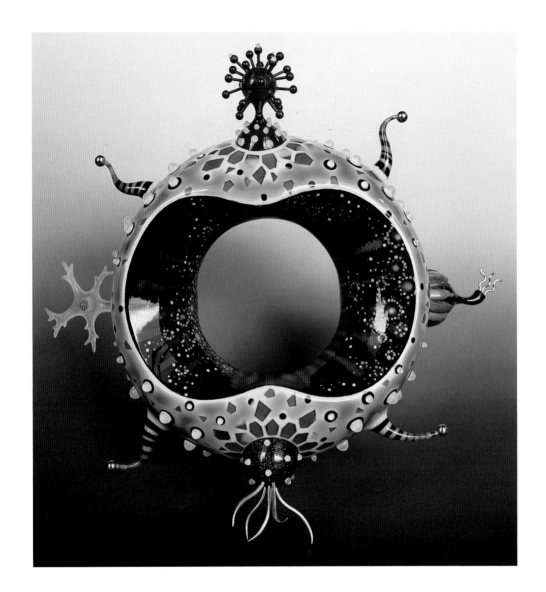

Peter Chang

Untitled, 2004

21.5 x 20 x 6 cm
Acrylic, resin, silver, PVC, lacquer; embedded,
laminated, lathe worked, carved, polished
PHOTO BY ARTIST
COLLECTION OF POWERHOUSE MUSEUM, SYDNEY, AUSTRALIA

Jeanet Metselaar
Untitled, 2001
12 x 10 x 3 cm
Leatherette, wood
PHOTO BY HANS KOSTERINK

Megan Auman

Poppies!, 2003

17 x 17 x 10 cm
Balloons, copper; hand fabricated, sewn
PHOTO BY NATHAN DUBE

Kanako Iida

Untitled, 2004

12 x 12 x 4.5 cm
Kimono silk; knitted
PHOTO BY HISATO TAKASHIMA

The traditional Japanese dress kimono has dropped out of daily use in modern times. I created this bracelet wishing to return life to this old cloth in other ways. By cutting and knitting the material, a totally new expression and style was born. **Kanako Iida**

Miriam Verbeek
Untitled, 2003
Each, 5 x 12 x 12 cm
Wool; felted
PHOTO BY ARTIST

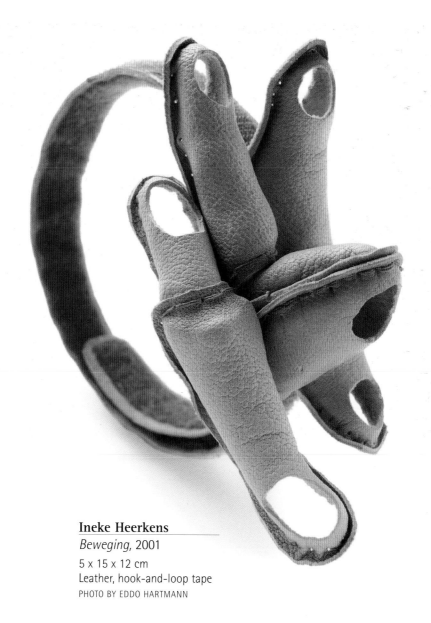

Ineke Heerkens

Beweging, 2001

5 x 15 x 12 cm
Leather, hook-and-loop tape
PHOTO BY EDDO HARTMANN

Bruce Clark

The Passion as Fashion—Wound, Bound,
and Wrapped Around, 2004

1 x 20 x 600 cm
Mesquite thorns, rubber, brass, metal leaf;
assembled
PHOTO BY ALICE VINSON

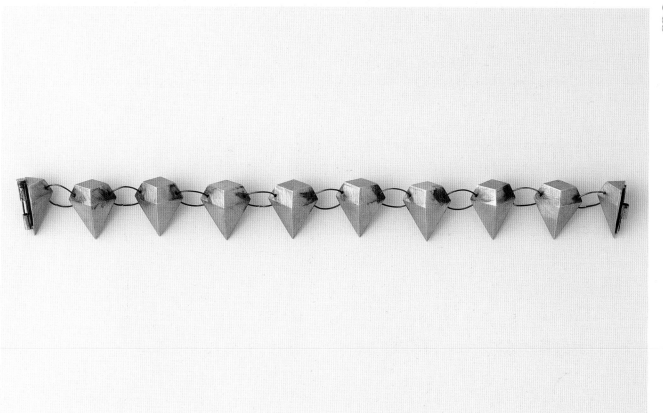

Philip Sajet
Parasit Bracelet, 1988

22 x 2.5 x 1.5 cm
Silver, 18-karat gold
PHOTO BY ARTIST

Julia Turner

Monster Truck Series #1, 2001

11 x 11 x 7 cm
Toy rubber truck tire, sterling silver; fabricated
PHOTO BY ARTIST

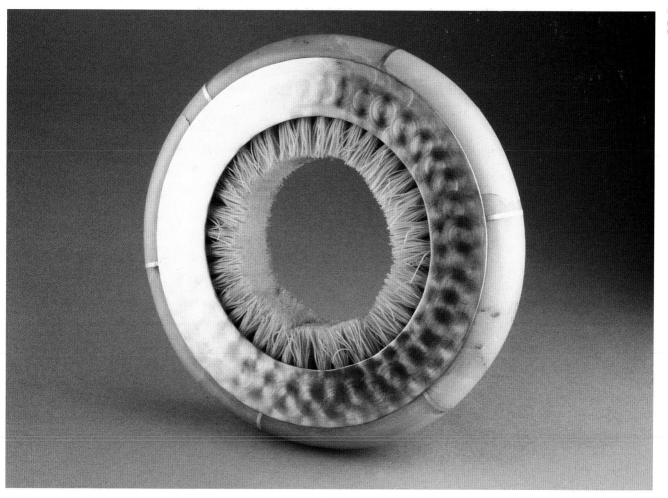

Mitchel T. Martin

Closer to Godliness, 2003

14 x 14 x 3 cm
Sterling silver, scrub brush,
soapstone; hand fabricated
PHOTO BY ARTIST

This bracelet addresses common
cultural belief through literal
and symbolic use of materials.
It is designed to be beautiful
and ironically uncomfortable.
Mitchel T. Martin

Michael Carberry

A Direct Response to the Material, 1997

15 x 14 x 4 cm
1-kilogram ingot of fine silver; hot forged

PHOTO BY ARTIST
COLLECTION OF ROYAL COLLEGE OF ART, LONDON, ENGLAND

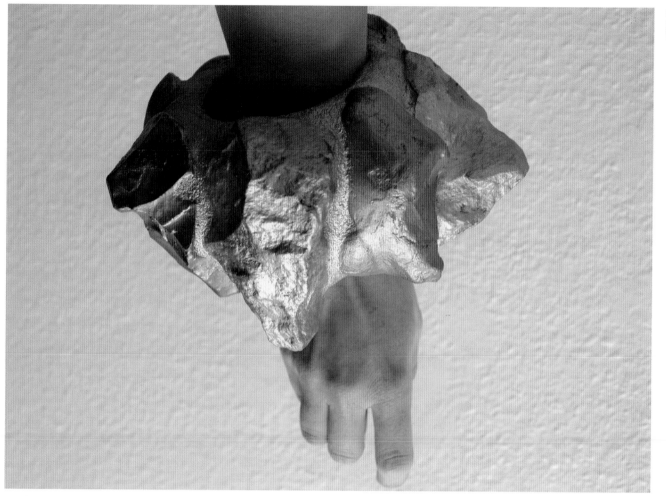

Roma Napoli and Black Sifichi

Bijoux Importable—Bracelet Made from Rocks, 1997

20 cm in diameter
Stones, plastic, metallic paint, cement; hand fabricated
PHOTO BY BOB JEUDY
COLLECTION OF BOB JEUDY

Kyoko Urino

Nature Study Series #123, 2000

Each, 10 x 10 x 1 cm
Twig, copper, white emerald, tourmaline, patina;
electroformed, hand fabricated, riveted
PHOTO BY KUNIYASU USUI

Kyoko Urino

*Nature Study Series
#325*, 2000

10 x 10 x 2 cm
Twig, copper, paint, patina,
gold leaf; electroformed,
hand fabricated, riveted
PHOTO BY KUNIYASU USUI

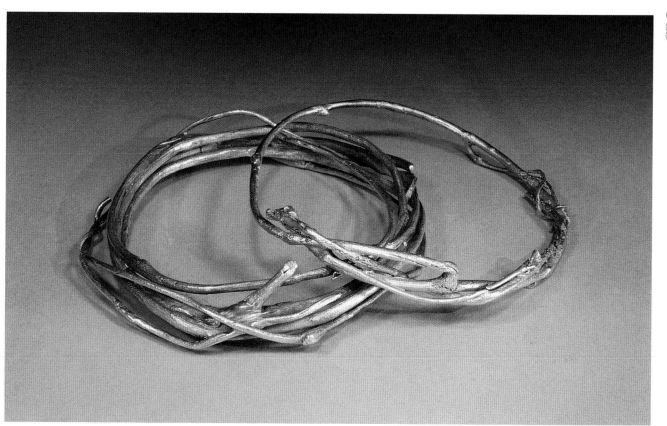

Heather Matwe
Willow Bracelets, 1999
Each, 7.3 x 1.9 x 7.5 cm
Sterling silver, patina; cast
PHOTO BY ARTIST

Kai Chan

Spots—Flower—Spring, 1985

26 x 20 x 24 cm
Rattan, fabric dye, wood, patina;
hand fabricated, glued

PHOTO BY ARTIST
COURTESY OF GALERIE ELENA LEE,
MONTREAL, CANADA

Patrick Marchal
Double You, 2001
Interior diameter, 6.8 cm
Recycled paper; laser cut
PHOTO BY ARTIST

K. Dana Kagrise

Ritual # 3 (detail), 2004

7.6 x 20.3 x 20.3 cm
Used coffee filters, cotton
batting, polyester thread; sewn
PHOTO BY ARTIST

Teresa Faris
Bracelet #2, 2004

4.5 x 14 cm in diameter
Latex; painted over form
PHOTO BY ARTIST

Jane Adam

Spiral Bangles, 1999

Average, 5 x 6 x 6 cm
Aluminum, dye; anodized, crazed

PHOTO BY JOËL DEGEN
COURTESY OF VELVET DA VINCI, SAN FRANCISCO, CALIFORNIA

Rose Sellery

Endorphic, 2004

8 x 8 x 1.7 cm
Sterling silver/22-karat gold
bimetal, patina; sawed,
anticlastic raising, formed, brushed
PHOTO BY ARTIST

Daniela Osterrieder

Turn Around, 2002

7.5 x 7.5 x 3.5 cm
Sterling silver; hand fabricated
PHOTO BY ARTIST

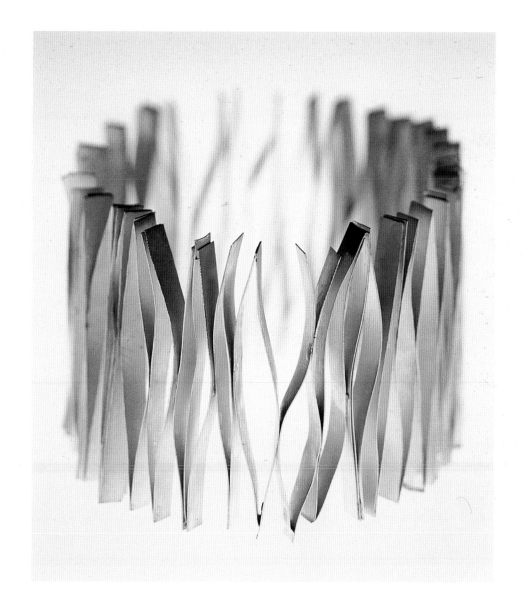

Sara Bacci

Morning, 2001

5 x 7 x 7 cm
Sterling silver; hand fabricated
PHOTO BY FEDERICO CAVICCHIOLI

Geoffrey D. Giles

Self Portrait, Cultivated Perception, 2003

17.8 x 17.8 x 2.2 cm
Sterling silver, 18-karat yellow gold, human hair, acrylic, photographs; hand fabricated, hollow formed, brushed finish, surface
embellishment, riveted, oxidized

PHOTO BY TAYLOR DABNEY
COLLECTION OF MINT MUSEUM OF CRAFT + DESIGN, CHARLOTTE, NORTH CAROLINA

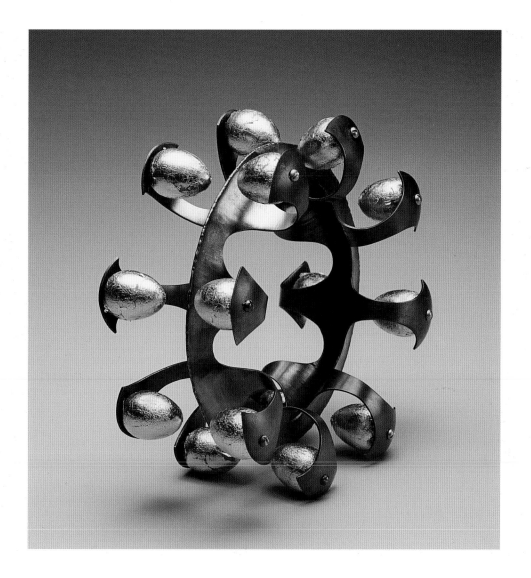

Evan H. Larson
Egg Drop, 2003
11.4 x 11.4 x 5 cm
Copper, wood; fold formed
PHOTO BY ARTIST

Todd Reed

Blue Chalcedony & *Raw Diamond Bracelet,* 2003

4.5 x 17 x 0.5 cm
18-karat yellow gold, 22-karat yellow gold, sterling silver,
natural diamond cubes, natural blue chalcedony, patina;
hand forged, hand fabricated, chisel set, brushed finish
PHOTO BY AZAD

Annette Clay

Untitled, 2000

8 x 8 x 4 cm
18-karat gold; hand fabricated, coiled
PHOTO BY ARTIST

Annamaria Zanella
Sabbie (Sands), 2003
7.5 x 3.5 cm in diameter
22-karat gold; hand fabricated
PHOTO BY LORENZO TRENTO

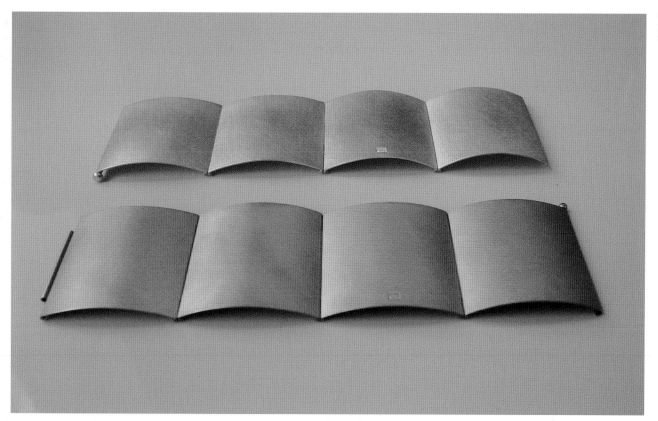

Daniela Osterrieder

Square, 2001

Closed, 5.5 x 5.5 x 4.5 cm
18-karat gold, sterling silver; hand fabricated
PHOTO BY ARTIST

Gina Pankowski

Tighra #3, 2002

8.5 x 8.5 x 2 cm
18-karat gold; cast, hand fabricated

PHOTO BY DOUGLAS YAPLE
COURTESY OF MOBILIA GALLERY,
CAMBRIDGE, MASSACHUSETTS

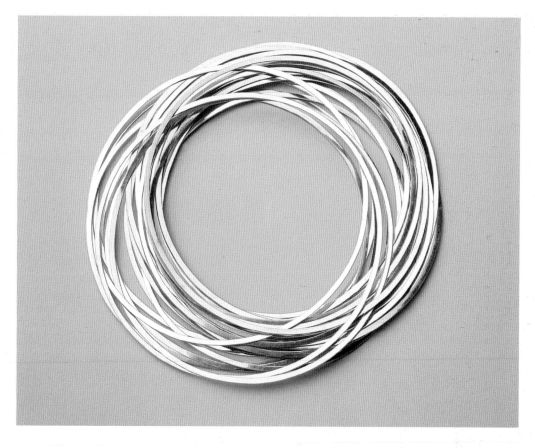

Claude Schmitz

Bracelet-Chain, 2003

As bracelet, 9.5 x 9.5 x 1 cm; as chain, 200 cm
18-karat gold; forged, polished
PHOTOS BY CHRISTIAN MOSAR

The 27 bracelets can be worn as either a
bracelet or a chain. By changing the
dimensions, not only the perception of
the weight is changed, but also the way
this piece can be worn. **Claude Schmitz**

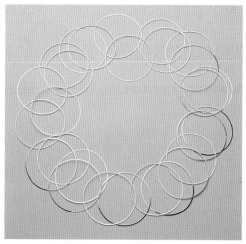

Stefano Marchetti
Untitled, 2003

7 x 7 x 9 cm
18-karat gold
PHOTO BY ROBERTO SORDI

Michael Becker

Untitled, 2003

6.5 cm in diameter
22-karat gold; hand fabricated
PHOTO BY WALTER KABERLAND

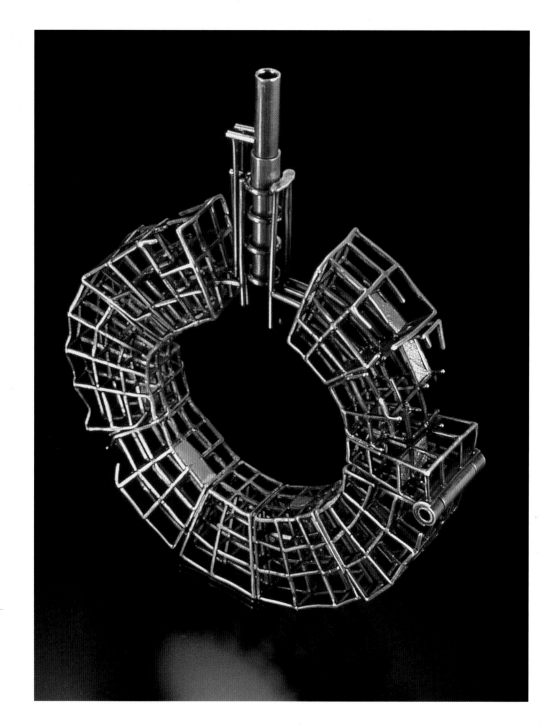

McIrvin Field-Sloan
Microcosm, 2003
15 x 11.3 x 2.5 cm
Sterling silver, 18-karat
gold, patina; cast, hand
fabricated
PHOTO BY ROBERT DIAMANTE

Ann L. Lumsden

Vacation, 2004

17 x 5 cm
Sterling silver, vintage postcards,
plastic and glass slide mounts, steel
spring bars; hand fabricated, riveted
PHOTO BY ARTIST

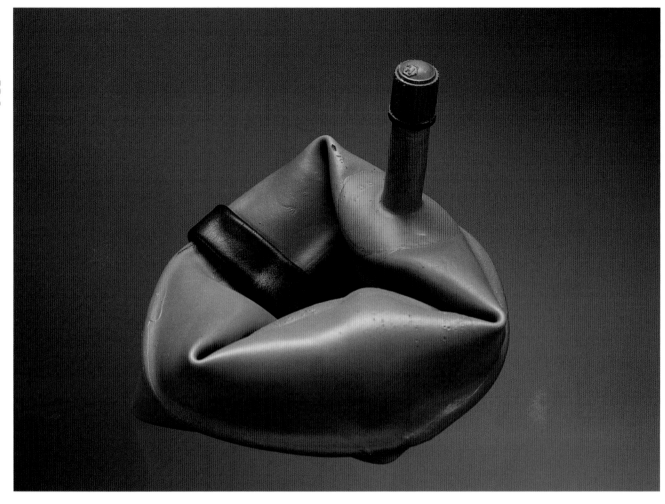

Philip J. Hoffman
Boys-n-Girls, 2003

6 x 8 x 4.5 cm
Rubber, plastic, oil paint; hand fabricated
PHOTO BY NORMAN WATKINS

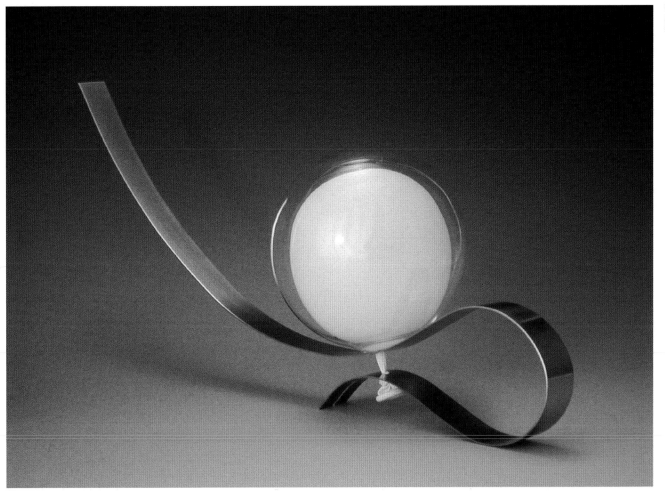

Ilin Hsu

Float #7, 2001

14 x 25 x 7.6 cm
Stainless steel, glass, balloon; hand fabricated,
cold connected
PHOTO BY ALIYA NAUMOFF

Mari Funaki

Untitled, 2004

9.2 x 8.9 x 1.1 cm
Mild steel; heat colored, fabricated

PHOTO BY TERENCE BOGUE
COURTESY OF GALLERY FUNAKI, MELBOURNE, AUSTRALIA

Rebecca Hannon
Spoon Bracelet, 2003

14 x 8 x 1.5 cm
Silver found object, patina;
milled, forged, slotted
PHOTO BY ARTIST

An easily recognized outline—
warm, comfortable, and simply
useful. Elongating the handle
created an elegant shape, but
rendered the spoon useless. By
bending it into a bracelet, a
dual-use object was created.
Rebecca Hannon

Alexandra Lisboa

Paradox, 2004

Left, 12 x 10.5 cm in diameter; right, 12 x 7 cm in diameter
Iron, paper, paint, paste; mechanically constructed, molded, hand fabricated
PHOTO BY ARTIST

Iron is heavy, hard, dense, and compact, but can also be soft, light, and smooth. It depends on...

Paper is soft, light, and smooth, but can also be heavy, hard, and dense. It depends on...

Alexandra Lisboa

Silke Trekel
Untitled, 2004
9 x 8 x 2 cm
Silver; hammered
PHOTO BY CHRISTOPH SANDIG

Masumi Kataoka
Untitled, 2004

10 x 3 x 10 cm
24-karat gold, human hair,
felt; knotted, soldered
PHOTO BY ARTIST

Yun Hee Kim
Angled, 2004
7.5 x 7.5 x 3.3 cm
Loofah, dye, resin
PHOTO BY MYUNG-WOOK HUH

Cathy Jarratt
Sea Anemones, 2004

6 x 16 x 16 cm
Coated copper wire; hand crocheted
PHOTO BY ARTIST

Jennifer Ramirez
Untitled, 2004
8.9 x 7.6 x 8.9 cm
Wool; needle felted
PHOTO BY NATALYA PINCHUK

Hanny Bürgin

Optical Designs, 2002

Each, 11 x 18 x 2.9 cm
Glass beads, cotton thread,
foam rubber; crocheted

PHOTOS BY A. LÜÖND
OSEC COLLECTION, BERNE, SWITZERLAND

Wim van Doorschodt

fruit de mer, 2000

Each, 2 x 10 x 10 cm
Acrylic, Corian; laminated, carved, filed
PHOTO BY TOM NOZ
COURTESY OF GALERIE RA, AMSTERDAM, NETHERLANDS

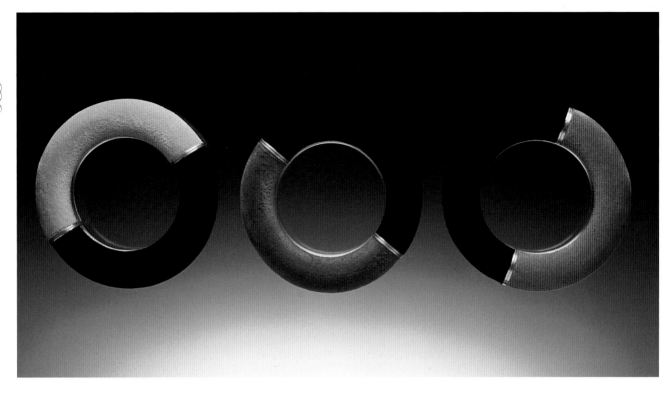

Daniel Jocz

Left, *Candy Wear: Chartreuse;* center, *Candy Wear: Blue;*
right, *Candy Wear: Orange,* 2001

Each, 10.2 x 10.2 x 2.5 cm
Silver, rayon flock, magnetic clasps; electroformed
PHOTO BY DEAN POWELL

Silke Trekel

Bracelet, 2002

2 x 11 cm in diameter
Balsa wood, paint; laminated
PHOTO BY HELGA SCHULZE-BRINKOP

Forms in architecture inspired this bracelet, which is almost more an object than it is jewelry. I keep returning to the square, the shape that has determined my formal language since the start of my involvement with jewelry. The square is primarily mirrored in the object's basic form, but also in its painted geometric ornamentation. It may be divided or rotated, sometimes appearing as a rhombus or as two triangular shapes.
Silke Trekel

Kirsten Clausager
Untitled, 2001

10 x 8 x 8 cm
Sterling silver; rolled,
soldered, bent
PHOTO BY OLE AKHOJ

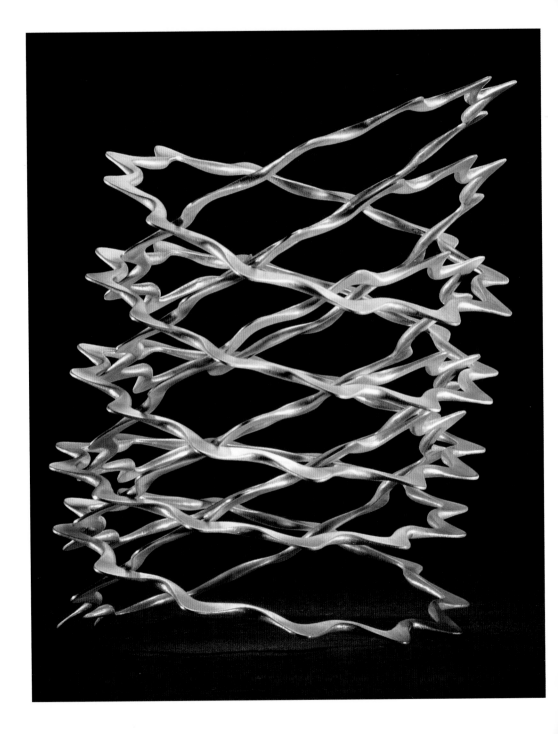

Sonia Morel

Untitled, 1997

6 x 9 x 9 cm
Sterling silver; hand fabricated, soldered,
laminated, oxidized
PHOTO BY THIERRY ZUFFEREY

Karl Fritsch
Untitled, 2003

13 x 13 x 3 cm
Sterling silver; cast, oxidized
PHOTO BY ARTIST

Dongchun Lee
Untitled, 2004

3.7 x 6.8 cm in diameter
Sterling silver, iron; cast
PHOTO BY KWANG-CHOON PARK

Mari Funaki

Untitled, 2004

7.9 x 9.2 x 1.8 cm
Mild steel; heat colored, fabricated

PHOTO BY TERENCE BOGUE
COURTESY OF GALLERY FUNAKI, MELBOURNE, AUSTRALIA

Zuzana Rudavska

Hematite Bracelet II, 2000

7.6 x 7.6 x 7.6 cm
Hematite, copper, sterling silver; laced
PHOTO BY GEORGE ERML

Adam Paxon
Mirror Bangle, 2003

12 x 12 x 2.8 cm
Acrylic; laminated,
hand carved, polished
PHOTO BY GRAHAM LEES

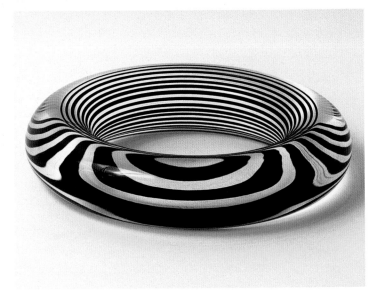

Friedrich Müller
Zebra, 2004

11.5 x 6.5 x 2.5 cm
Acrylic; turned, engraved, polished
PHOTO BY ARTIST

Kepa Karmona
20 cents, 2004
6.2 x 7.9 x 8.6 cm
Plastic coin packages; assembled
PHOTO BY ARTIST

April Higashi

Untitled, 2002

Largest, 9 x 9 x 4 cm
Newspaper, magazines, fabric,
lacquer; collaged

PHOTO BY HAP SAKWA
COURTESY OF MICHAEL MARTIN GALLERY,
SAN FRANCISCO, CALIFORNIA

Manuel Vilhena

Untitled, 2001

12 x 12 x 3 cm
Oak, steel; hand fabricated
PHOTO BY ARTIST

Peter Chang

Untitled, 2000

16.5 x 17 x 8 cm
Acrylic, resin, silver; embedded mosaic,
thermoformed, lathe turned, carved,
polished

PHOTO BY SHANNON TOFTS
PRIVATE COLLECTION

Philip Sajet
Water Bracelet, 1991

15 x 4 x 1 cm
Enamel, silver, 18-karat gold
PHOTO BY ARTIST

ROY

Rubber Duckie Bracelet (Homage to Fania), 2004

6.4 x 12.7 x 12.7 cm
Silver, nylon, found objects
PHOTO BY DEAN POWELL

Pavel Herynek
Constructed Paper Bracelets Series, 2004
Each, 9.5 x 10 x 9.8 cm
Cartons, postcards, steel; cut, constructed
PHOTO BY MARKÉTA ONDRUŠKOVÁ

Marjorie Schick

Riser Armlet on Base, 2004

Base, 11.4 x 29.8 x 29.8 cm;
armlet, 31.4 x 14.8 x 10.4 cm
Wood, plastic laminate, paint;
constructed, cut, pegged
PHOTOS BY GARY POLLMILLER

Flóra Vági

Untitled, 2003

Each, 4 x 10 cm in diameter
Wood, pigment, steel; hand fabricated,
sawed, burned, riveted
PHOTO BY FEDERICO CAVICCHIOLI

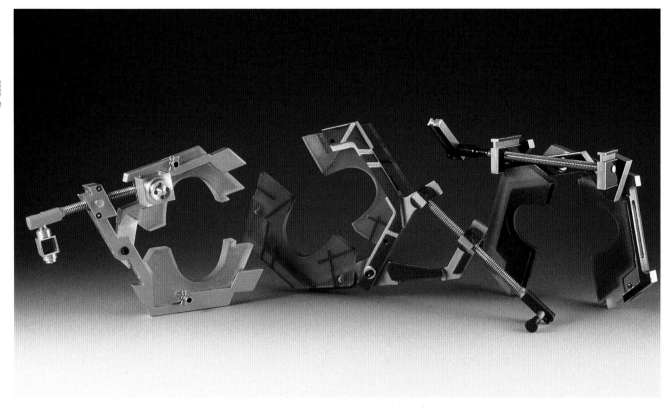

Frankie Flood
¹/₄-20 Bracelet Series, 2000

Each, 11.4 x 20.3 x 3.2 cm
Aluminum, acrylic, enamel paint,
stainless steel; fabricated,
machined, cold connected
PHOTO BY ARTIST

I utilize industrial processes—machining, stamping, anodizing, and powder coating—to create one-of-a-kind functional objects. Having worked in an industrial setting, I observed machinists highly capable in their fields, but unable to appreciate the artistic value of their methods and techniques. **Frankie Flood**

Brian Roberts

Exfoliatus, 2001

8.3 x 10.2 x 5.1 cm
Galvanized steel, stainless steel, mild steel;
hand fabricated, riveted, tabbed

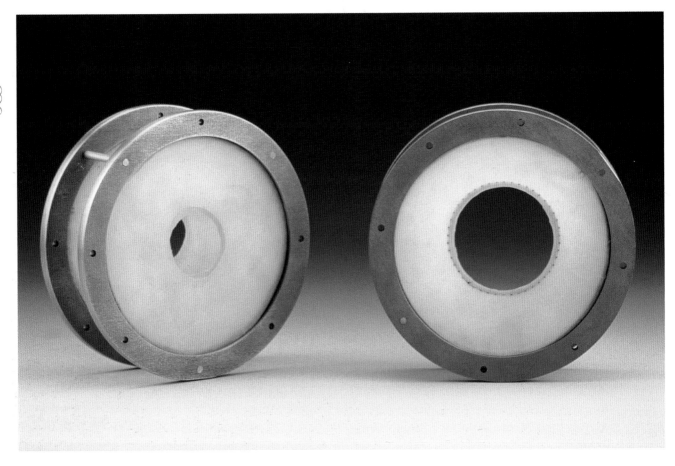

Harley J. McDaniel

Taut, 2003

Each, 13 x 13 x 7.8 cm
Stainless steel, latex; machined,
hand fabricated
PHOTO BY JEFF SABO

Ilin Hsu
Float #9, 2001
25 x 10 x 25 cm
Nickel silver, balloons;
hand fabricated, cold
connected
PHOTO BY ALIYA NAUMOFF

Erik Urbschat

Turnus, 2004

Largest, 8 x 8 x 1.5 cm
Sterling silver; forged, assembled
PHOTO BY ARTIST

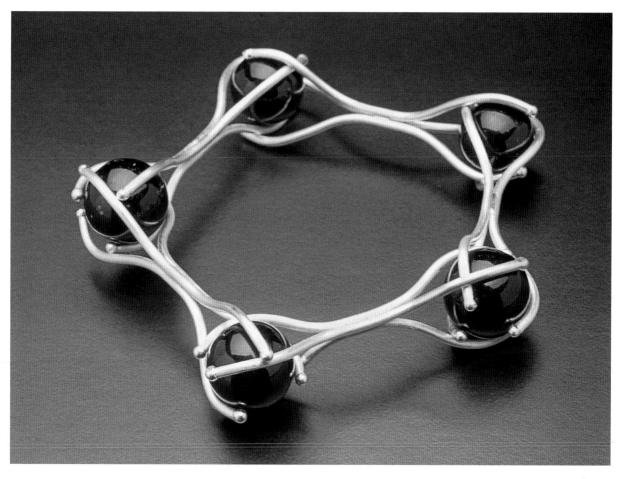

Jessica J. Bates

What a Marble-ous Bracelet, 2004

6 cm in diameter
Sterling silver, marbles; hand fabricated,
tension set

PHOTOS BY KEITH MEISER

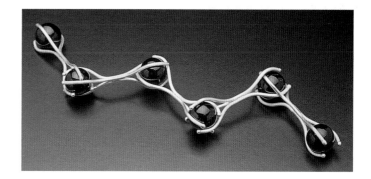

Natalya Pinchuk
Untitled, 2003

10 x 10 x 5 cm
Copper, enamel, plastic flowers
PHOTO BY ARTIST

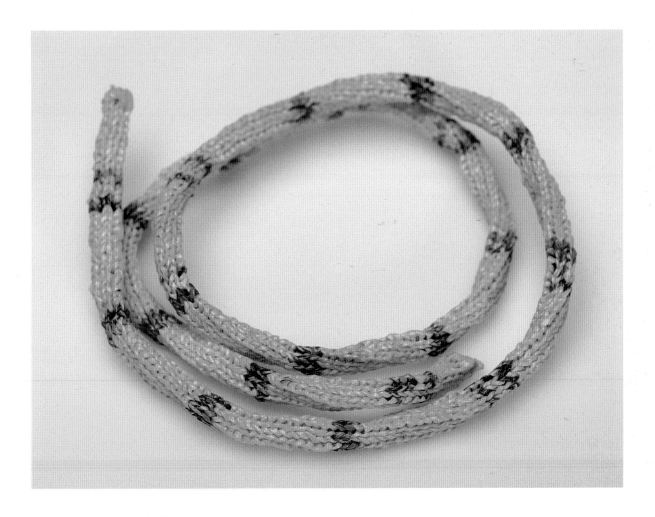

Shelley Norton

Untitled, 2004

1 x 40 x 1 cm
Plastic bags; cut, knitted
PHOTO BY JOHN COLLIE

My work centers around how we construct meaning. I decided to play with our culturally constructed stories about what jewelry should be. I wanted to create fun, colorful pieces that would engage the viewer and collapse barriers...to draw attention to established knowledge, while at the same time looking at new ways of seeing and comprehending.

Shelley Norton

Felieke van der Leest

Hare O'Harix and His 6 Carrots, 2004

3.5 x 30 x 4 cm

Yarns, felt, 10-karat gold, rubber, purchased toy; crocheted, fabricated, cast

PHOTO BY EDDO HARTMANN

You can wear the carrot bracelet, and leave the hare at home.
Felieke van der Leest

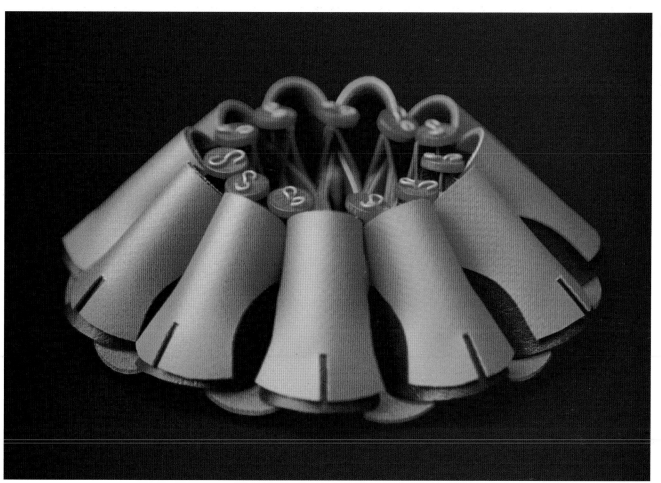

Jeanet Metselaar
Untitled, 2003
4 x 13 x 6 cm
Leatherette, polyester, wood
PHOTO BY HANS KOSTERINK

Cristina Dias
Carnivora #3, 2004

13 x 15 x 6 cm
Rubber, plastic, spring
steel, pigments; cast,
dipped, assembled
PHOTO BY ARTIST

Carnivorous plants, especially the sundew species, fascinate me. Their beautiful shapes and colors are so inextricably linked to their function to allure. My work recreates these tantalizing forms and transforms them into playful, colorful pieces. I incorporate spring steel and magnets attached to rubber to allow my jewelry to grab onto your arm or stick to your skin; then, the relation between the body and my jewelry becomes evident.
Cristina Dias

Caz Guiney

Imitate—Flexible Bracelets, 2000

3 x 8 x 8 cm

Acrylic, stainless steel springs; machine cut

PHOTO BY ANITA BEANEY

These bracelets create an austere yet playful beauty out of commonplace, synthetic materials. They are simple objects that speak profoundly about the possibilities of repetition, the interconnectedness of two-dimensional and three-dimensional geometry, and their own purpose: as objects of desire, contemplation, and adornment. **Caz Guiney**

Nel Linssen
Untitled, 1986

Each, 5 x 8 cm in diameter
Paper, elastic; folded

PHOTO BY PETER BLIEK

Inês Nunes
Untitled, 2002
26 cm in diameter
Roll of adhesive tape; readymade
PHOTO BY FREDERICO AZEVEDO AND CLAUDIO FERREIRA

Kai Chan

Florentine Cop, 1985

34 x 4 x 4 cm
Teak, cherry, fabric dye, elastic,
lacquer; turned, glued

PHOTO BY ARTIST
COURTESY OF GALERIE RA,
AMSTERDAM, NETHERLANDS

K.C. Calum

Untitled, 2004

13 x 13 x 2.5 cm
Wood, rubber, paint; hand fabricated
PHOTO BY ARTIST

Jun Park

The Egocentric, 2004

4.5 x 8.7 x 6.2 cm
Sterling silver, paint; cast, oxidized, hinged
PHOTO BY MYUNG-WOOK HUH
COURTESY OF THE ROMAN CATHOLIC CHURCH,
HYUNMOK, KOREA

Salima Thakker

Modular Bracelet 2, 2003

4.5 x 18 x 0.7 cm
18-karat yellow gold, sterling silver,
patina; hand fabricated
PHOTO BY PHOTOLOGY

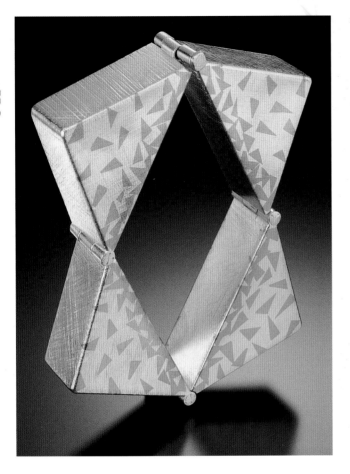

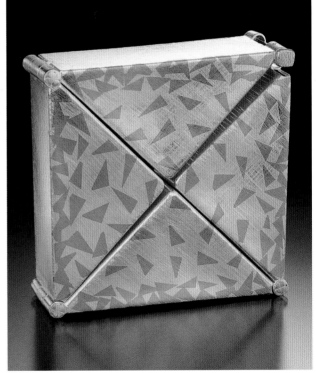

Marguerite Manteau Chiang

Square, 2003

24.1 x 3.2 x 20.3 cm
Sterling silver, 24-karat gold, 18-karat gold,
14-karat gold; kum boo, hand fabricated,
file finished

PHOTOS BY HAP SAKWA

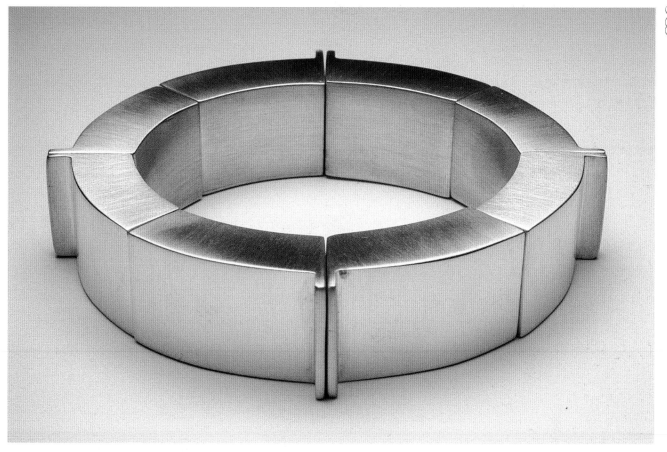

Gun Thor

Oval One, 2003

7.5 cm in diameter
Silver, stainless steel springs;
cast, hand fabricated
PHOTO BY JOËL DEGEN

My bracelets evolved from the search for a design unbroken by a clasp, which would also be easy for the wearer to put on and take off. The stainless steel springs—specially made for me—offer the ideal solution. They expand to slide the bracelet over the hand, then contract again to fit around the wrist. **Gun Thor**

Pavel Herynek
Chicago Bracelets Series, 2004
Right, 10.2 x 7.2 x 7 cm
Steel; cut, filed, hand fabricated
PHOTO BY MARKÉTA ONDRUŠKOVÁ

addam
Venus Fly Wrap, 2004
12.4 x 12.4 x 9.4 cm
Sterling silver; hand
fabricated, soldered
PHOTO BY VICTOR FRANCE

Annamaria Zanella

Fado, 2004

7.5 x 7.5 x 3 cm

22-karat gold; hand fabricated

PHOTO BY LORENZO TRENTO

In these bracelets you can see the changing play of light and shadow, or brightness and darkness, the day and the night sides of jewelry, which is also sculpture. They reveal happiness and sorrow, pain, and the affirmation of life.

Annamaria Zanella

Graziano Visintin
Bracelet, 1990
7 x 7 x 1.2 cm
18-karat yellow gold
PHOTO BY LORENZO TRENTO

Giovanni Corvaja
Untitled, 1999

9 x 9 x 4.5 cm
18-karat gold, 22-karat gold;
niello, constructed
PHOTO BY ARTIST

Christa Lühtje
Untitled, 2003

6.7 cm in diameter
22-karat gold, rock crystal
PHOTO BY EVA JÜNGER

Lanelle W. Keyes
Entwine, 2002

7.5 x 7.5 x 5.5 cm
Iron, 22-karat gold; twisted, knotted
PHOTO BY DOUG YAPLE

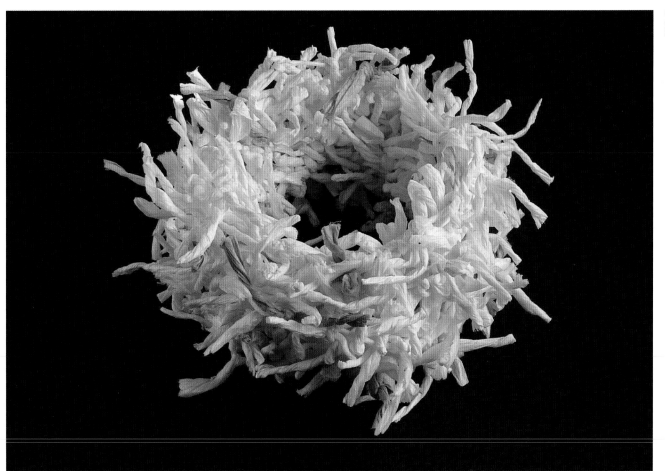

Meiri Ishida

Untitled, 2004

6 x 14 x 14 cm
Sterling silver, paper;
hand fabricated

Carolina Tell

Untitled, 2001

8 x 9 x 7 cm
Corrugated cardboard, thread,
plastic beads; hand fabricated, sewn
PHOTO BY MELANIE SEILER

K. Dana Kagrise
Ritual #1, 2004

10.2 x 20.3 x 20.3 cm
Used coffee filters, cotton batting,
polyester thread; sewn
PHOTO BY ARTIST

357

Eve Iris Bennett

Tooth, 2004

8.3 x 8.3 x 1.3 cm
Sterling silver, fossilized shark teeth,
liver of sulphur patina; hand fabricated,
photoetched, prong set
PHOTO BY ROBERT DIFRANCO

Brian Roberts

Baby Blue, 2002

11.5 x 11.5 x 3.8 cm
Blue popcorn, steel; carved, riveted
PHOTO BY JEFFREY SABO

I investigate materials that have a relationship to agriculture, pursuing the potential of these materials to contain visual and metaphoric expression within their physical matter. **Brian Roberts**

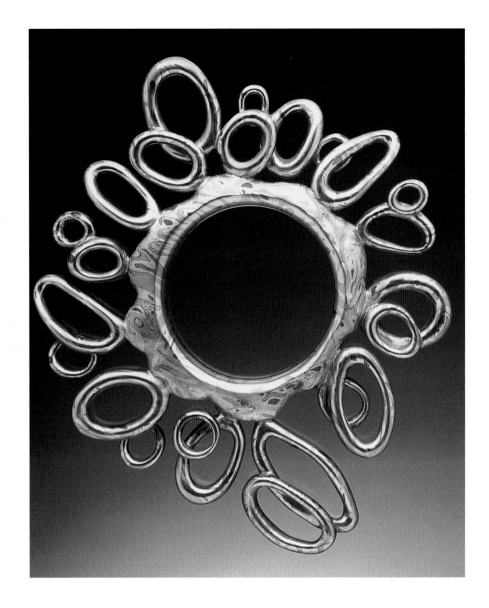

Daniel Jocz

Aluminum Three Ways: Bubble Bath, 2004

17.8 cm in diameter
Aluminum; carved, anodized
PHOTO BY DEAN POWELL

Barbara Stutman

Untitled, 2004

4 x 19 x 19 cm
Polypropylene, monofilament, dye;
crocheted

PHOTO BY ANTHONY MCLEAN
COURTESY OF GALERIE NOEL GUYOMARC'H,
MONTREAL, CANADA

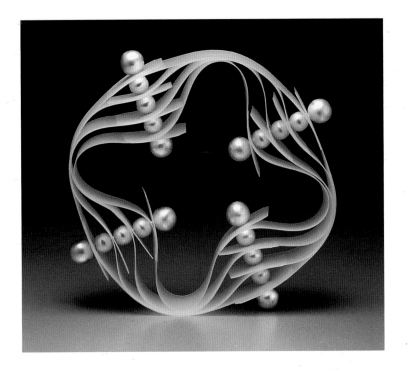

Hyeseung Shin
Plastic Bracelet I, 2003

8 x 8 x 2 cm
Plastic, sterling silver
PHOTOS BY MYUNG WOOK HUH

My use of a nonprecious material does not mean that I am not serious about the form of my jewelry. I believe the material shows the possibility for jewelry to be playful. Like a toy, it is accessible to the touch, its playfulness enhanced by the incorporation of color.
Hyeseung Shin

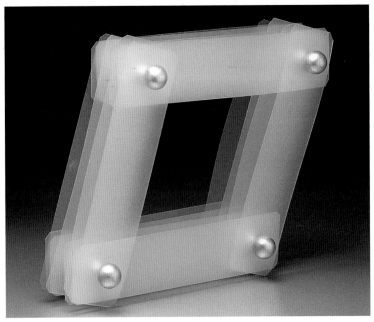

Sarah Enoch
impression, 2001
2 x 9.5 x 10 cm
Acrylic; thermoformed
PHOTO BY TOM NOZ

Fabiana Gadano

Intonso Bracelet, 2003

14 x 4 x 14 cm
Sterling silver, kozo paper, copper,
heat patina; anticlastic raising

PHOTO BY PATRICIO GATTI
COURTESY OF VELVET DA VINCI,
SAN FRANCISCO, CALIFORNIA

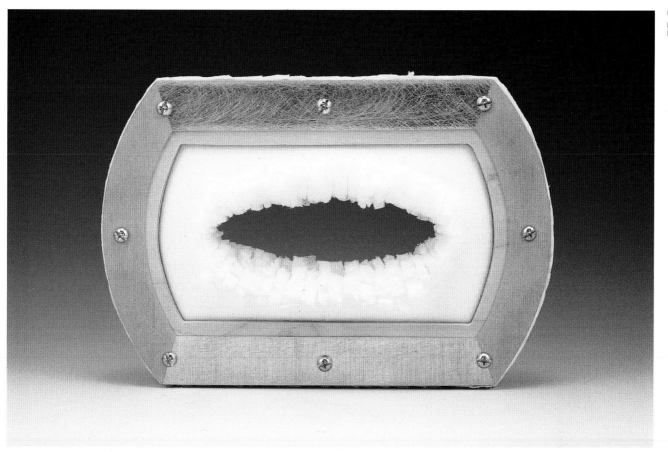

Gary J. Schott
Caution: Enter Slowly, 2004

10 x 15 x 3 cm
Aluminum, plywood, tissue,
steel nuts and bolts;
hand fabricated
PHOTO BY ARTIST

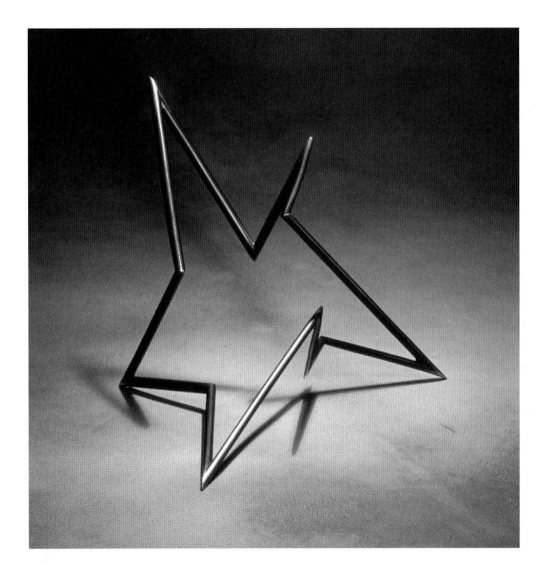

Susan R. Ewing

Prague Star Series: Bracelet I, 1999

12.5 x 12.5 x 7.5 cm
Sterling silver; hand fabricated, oxidized
PHOTO BY MARTIN TUMA

Madelyn C. Ricks
Deco Bracelet, 2004

14 x 14 x 5 cm
Glass beads, thread, polymer clay,
leather; peyote stitched, lined
PHOTO BY JERRY ANTHONY

Barbara Paganin

12 Valve, 1999

9.5 cm in diameter
18-karat gold, silver, pearls;
hand fabricated, oxidized
PHOTO BY ALBINO FECCHIO

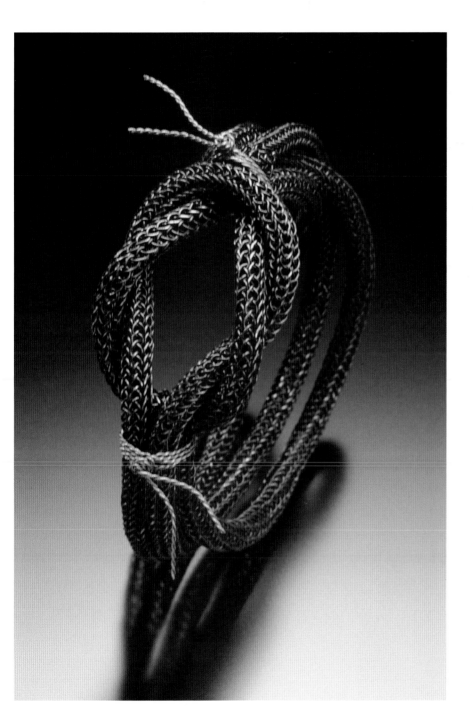

Lanelle W. Keyes
Hercules Knot, 2002

7.5 x 7.5 x 3 cm
Iron, 18-karat gold;
hand knitted, knotted
PHOTO BY DOUG YAPLE

Jin-Soon Woo

Untitled, 1995

7.4 cm in diameter
Sterling silver; hand fabricated
PHOTO BY YOUNG-IL KIM

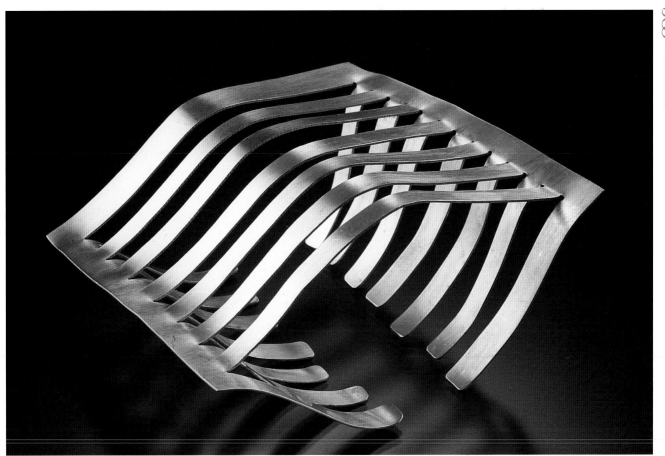

Anne M. Heinz
Weaving, 2003

6.5 x 13 cm
Sterling silver; fabricated
PHOTO BY LARRY SANDERS
PRIVATE COLLECTION

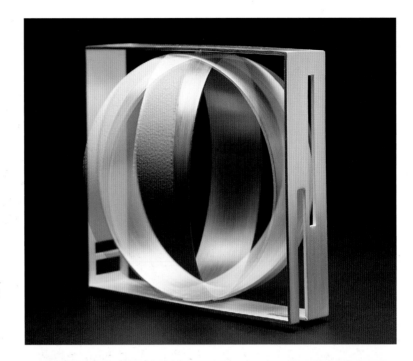

Myoung-Sun Lee
Light & *Shadow 1*, 2002
6.5 x 7.5 x 1.5 cm
Sterling silver
PHOTO BY MYUNG-WOOK HUH

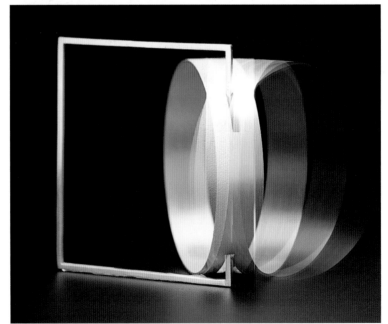

Myoung-Sun Lee
Light & *Shadow 2*, 2002
6.5 x 6.5 x 1.5 cm
Sterling silver
PHOTO BY MYUNG-WOOK HUH

Ji-Hee Hong

Balance, 2004

7.5 x 7 x 3.2 cm
Sterling silver, copper; soldered,
hand fabricated

PHOTO BY KWANG-CHOON PARK

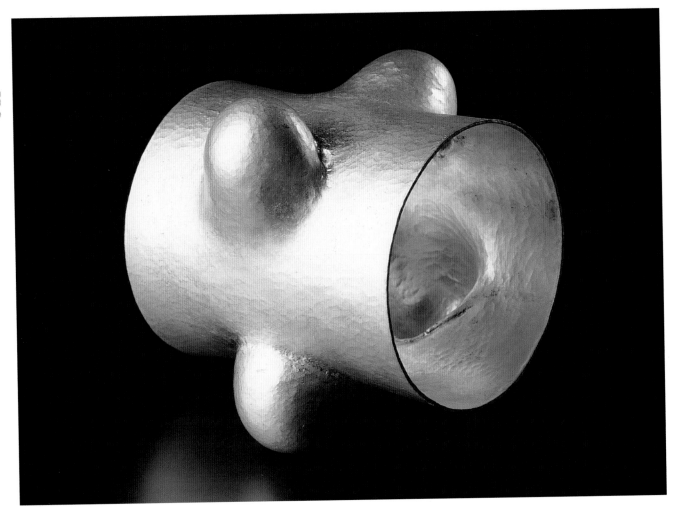

Mizuko Yamada
Tactile Bracelet, 2000

12 x 12 x 9 cm
Copper, silver; hammered, plated
PHOTO BY TOSHIHIDE KAJIHARA

Dorothy Hogg MBE

Bangle with 100 Rings, 1999

8 x 9 x 2 cm
Sterling silver; anticlastic
raising, hammered
PHOTO BY JOHN K. MCGREGOR

One hundred hammered rings move
freely around the form, massaging
the hand as the bracelet is worn.
Dorothy Hogg MBE

Sara Lillis

Up In Smoke, 2004

15 x 17 x 10 cm
Sterling silver, antique wooden
pipes, patina, epoxy; hand
fabricated, riveted, oxidized, glued
PHOTOS BY YUKO YAGISAWA

This piece is one in a series
in which the dominant
elements—in this case
tobacco pipes—conventionally
categorized as male or
masculine, are arranged in
a refreshing new way that is
strikingly female or feminine.
Sara Lillis

Juan Carlos Caballero-Peréz

Stitches, 2004

15.2 cm in diameter
Fine silver, sterling silver, felt, stainless steel,
gold plate; hand fabricated, fused, hammer
formed, stamped, oxidized
PHOTO BY DAN NEUBERGER

Amy Reeves

Quiver, 2003

12.7 x 12.7 x 30.5 cm
Sterling silver, stainless steel;
cast, hand fabricated
PHOTO BY ARTIST

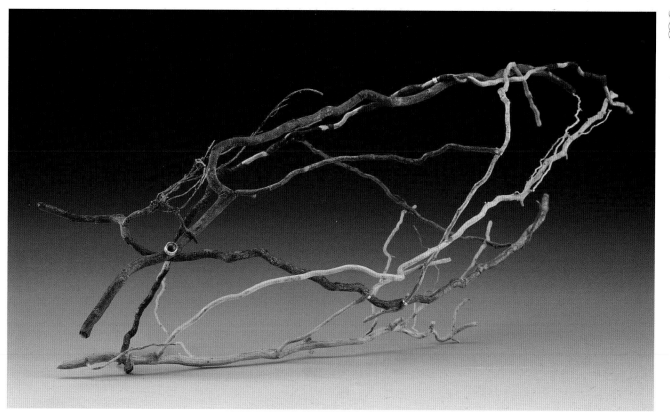

Pauline Dennis
Veination, 2004

9 x 29 x 10 cm
Roots, sterling silver, tiger's eye;
riveted, hand fabricated
PHOTO BY JEFF SABO

Eva Tesarik

The Cloned Bears NR.
3743–3762, 2004

2.5 x 13 cm
Sterling silver
PHOTO BY JUDITH WIESER-HUBER

Lucia Moure
Chasing Tails, 2003
2 x 15 cm in diameter
Brass, gold; soldered, cast
PHOTO BY ARTIST

Margaux Lange

36 Giggles, 2004

2 x 3 x 17.5 cm
Sterling silver, plastic, epoxy resin;
hand fabricated

PHOTO BY AZAD
COURTESY OF JULIE ARTISANS' GALLERY,
NEW YORK, NEW YORK

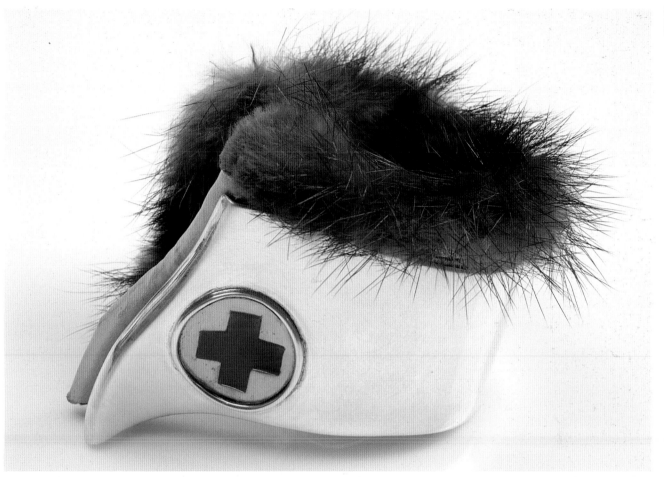

DuWayne Blankley

Mink Cuff, 2003

6 x 14.5 cm
Silver, mink, pink leather,
plastic, battery, LED; hand
fabricated, sewn
PHOTO BY MARGO GEIST

I enjoy playing with multiple materials using traditional construction techniques to evoke forms of fashion and curiosity. **DuWayne Blankley**

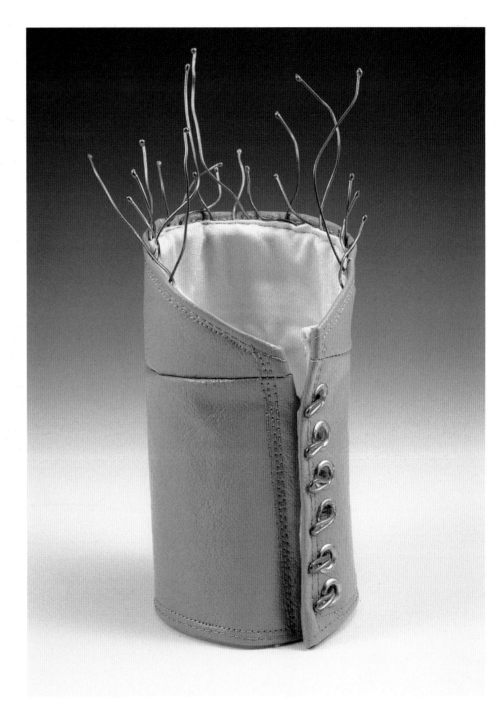

Kim Marissa Shay
Vinyl Mystique, 2003

12.7 x 6.4 x 6.4 cm
Vinyl, fabric, brass; sewn, riveted
PHOTO BY ARTIST

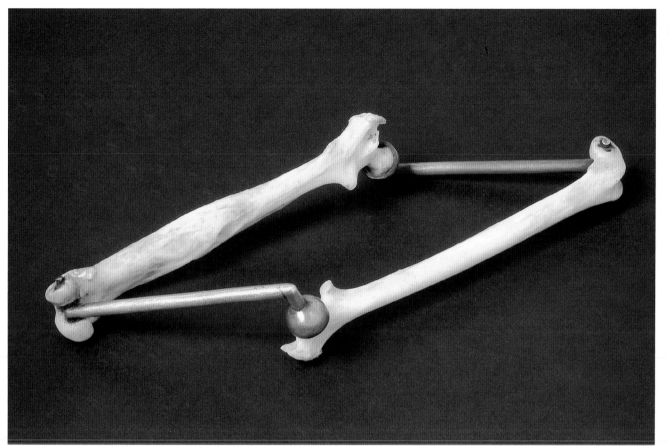

Teresa Milheiro

Prosthesis, 2002

2.5 x 6.5 x 9 cm
Bones, silver; hand fabricated,
oxidized
PHOTO BY LUIS PAIS

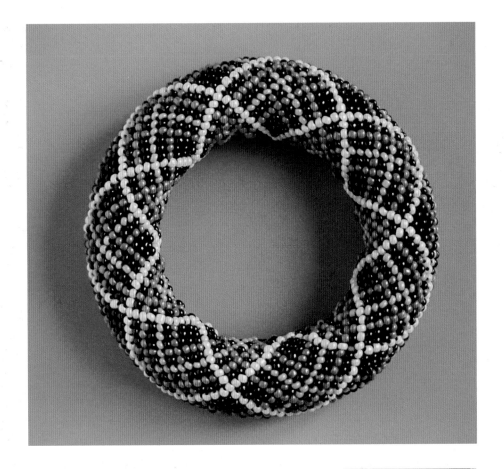

Hanny Bürgin

Optical Designs, 2002

Each, 9.5 x 17 cm
Glass beads, cotton thread, foam rubber; crocheted

PHOTOS BY A. LÜÖND
OSEC COLLECTION, BERNE, SWITZERLAND

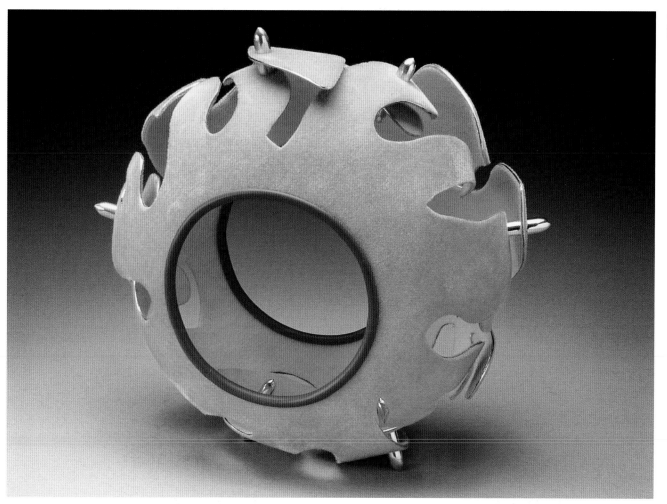

Daniel Jocz
Aluminum Three Ways: Chartreuse Explo, 2003

15.2 cm in diameter
Aluminum, rayon flock
PHOTO BY DEAN POWELL

Miriam Verbeek
ball bracelet, 2003
6 x 10 x 10 cm
Wool; felted, crocheted
PHOTO BY ARTIST

Arthur David Hash
Bag Series Bracelet, 2004
20.3 x 16.5 x 11.4 cm
Cast foam, dye
PHOTO BY ARTIST

Peter Chang

Untitled, 1999

6 x 16.5 cm in diameter
Acrylic, resin, silver, lacquer; thermoformed,
profile molded, carved, polished

PHOTO BY ARTIST
PRIVATE COLLECTION

Karen McCreary
Radial Pulse Emitter, 1994

16 x 16 x 4 cm
Acrylic, nickel silver, electronics, light;
hand carved, fabricated
PHOTO BY ARTIST

Ilin Hsu

Float #4, 2000

17 x 12 x 15 cm
Sterling silver, spring
steel, glass, balloon;
hand fabricated, cold
connected
PHOTOS BY ALIYA NAUMOFF

I do not create jewelry to glamorize the body. The human form is the only place where my work can reside. My work is a mental thing, and our body is a tangible existence of mind and spirit. I want the wearer to be aware of the work's actuality, like the ups and downs of our lives, and to sense its insecurity and surprises. Glass balls and balloons are all subtle humor to convey this idea. As fragile as it may seem, the invisible element of air holds every single part together to symbolize the unseen faith and hope around us. **Ilin Hsu**

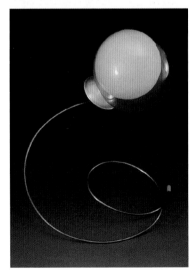

Susan May
Big Bangle, 2003
13 x 13 x 7 cm
Sterling silver
PHOTO BY ARTIST

Laura Aragon

Untitled, 2003

Left, 12.7 x 12.7 x 5 cm; right, 10.2 x 10.2 x 5 cm
Thermoplastic, silver; cut, riveted, heat folded
PHOTO BY RACHELLE THIEWES

Karen Bachmann
Black Egg Cuff, 2004

7 x 9 x 3.5 cm
Lucite, ebony; hand carved,
polished
PHOTO BY ARTIST

With thermoformed plastics, pressure applied to warm material has a deep and immediate effect: geometrical forms change within seconds from rigid plastic elements into unique objects. By shifting and condensing the mass, the piece gains its identity. Single elements become closely connected by having formed each other and having left their imprints behind.
Sarah Enoch

Sarah Enoch
unity, 2001
2 x 10 x 10 cm
Corian; thermoformed
PHOTO BY TOM NOZ

Karen-Sam Norgard
Black and White Bracelet, 2004
15 x 11 x 4 cm
Polymer clay; hand formed, caned
PHOTO BY DAVID LEE GOLDEN

Kirsten Clausager
Untitled, 2002
2 x 11 x 11 cm
Sterling silver; cast, soldered
PHOTO BY OLE AKHOJ

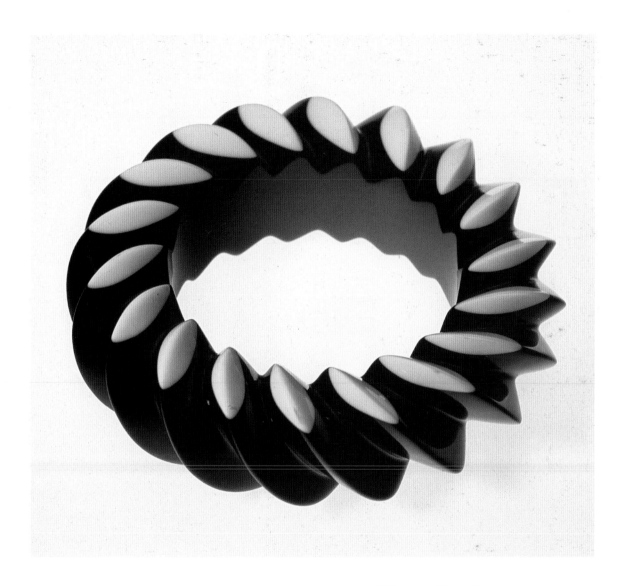

Wim van Doorschodt

Untitled, 1996

3 x 10.5 x 10.5 cm
Acrylic; laminated, carved

PHOTO BY TON WERKHOVEN
COURTESY OF GALERIE RA, AMSTERDAM, NETHERLANDS

Karl Fritsch
Untitled, 2003

6 x 9 x 4 cm
Sterling silver; cast, oxidized
PHOTO BY ARTIST

Yeonkyung Kim
Bracelet, 2000
15 cm in diameter
Leather
PHOTO BY ARTIST

Françoise A. Sands

Untitled, 2002

8 x 9.5 cm in diameter
24-karat gold plate, silver, copper;
hand fabricated

PHOTO BY GEORGE POST

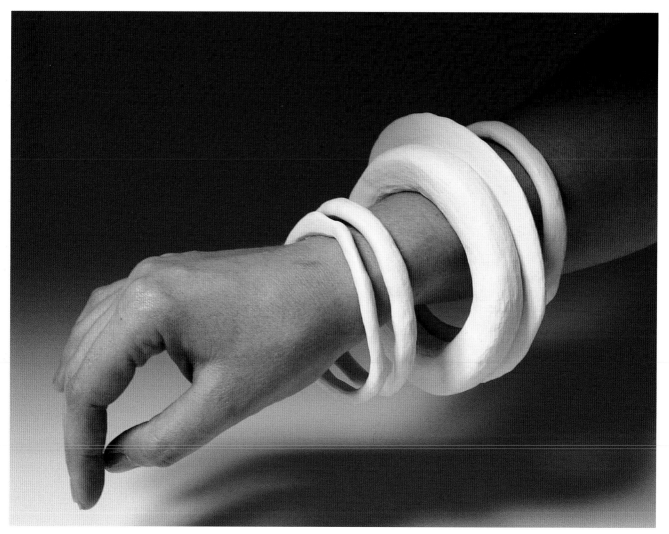

Randy Long
White Flow Bracelets, 2004
Largest, 11.5 x 11.5 x 1.6 cm
Two-part plastic; cast, carved
PHOTO BY ARTIST

Contributing Artists

Acknowledgments

Deepest appreciation goes to Charon Kransen, who liberally shared his substantial knowledge, keen insights, and passion for jewelry with us. His succinct observations and unflagging energy during the jurying deliberations made this demanding process a pleasure.

Without the 1,200 jewelers and artists who generously submitted imagery of their work, this book could never have been created. We are grateful for their enthusiasm in sharing their jewelry with Lark Books and its readers.

Thanks also to the galleries, guilds, and schools that tirelessly dedicate themselves to supporting and enriching the field of studio jewelry. They contributed immensely to creating a buzz and disseminating information about this book.

We're indebted to top-notch editorial assistants—Delores Gosnell, Dawn Dillingham, and Rosemary Kast—whose meticulous attention to detail kept the project oiled and running smoothly. Thank you also to Susan McBride for her impeccable sense of design in laying out this book, and to Shannon Yokeley and Lance Wille for their unfailing good humor during the book's production.

Marthe Le Van and **Nathalie Mornu**